Women's work 1840–1940

New Studies in Economic and Social History

Edited for the Economic History Society by
Michael Sanderson
University of East Anglia, Norwich

This series, specially commissioned by the Economic History Society, provides a guide to the current interpretations of the key themes of economic and social history in which advances have recently been made or in which there has been significant debate.

In recent times economic and social history has been one of the most flourishing areas of historical study. This has mirrored the increasing relevance of the economic and social sciences both in a student's choice of career and in forming a society at large more aware of the importance of these issues in their everyday lives. Moreover specialist interests in business, agricultural and welfare history, for example, have themselves burgeoned and there has been an increased interest in the economic development of the wider world. Stimulating as these scholarly developments have been for the specialist, the rapid advance of the subject and the quantity of new publications make it difficult for the reader to gain an overview of particular topics, let alone the whole field.

New Studies in Economic and Social History is intended for students and their teachers. It is designed to introduce them to fresh topics and to enable them to keep abreast of recent writing and debates. All the books in the series are written by a recognised authority in the subject, and the arguments and issues are set out in a critical but unpartisan fashion. The aim of the series is to survey the current state of scholarship, rather than to provide a set of prepackaged conclusions.

The series has been edited since its inception in 1968 by Professors M. W. Flinn, T. C. Smout and L. A. Clarkson, and is currently edited by Dr Michael Sanderson. From 1968 it was published by Macmillan as *Studies in Economic History*, and after 1974 as *Studies in Economic and Social History*. From 1995 *New Studies in Economic and Social History* is being published on behalf of the Economic History Society by Cambridge University Press. This new series includes some of the titles previously published by Macmillan as well as new titles, and reflects the ongoing development throughout the world of this rich seam of history.

For a full list of titles in print, please see the end of the book.

Women's work 1840–1940

Prepared for the Economic History Society by

Elizabeth Roberts
University of Lancaster

Published by the Press Syndicate of the University of Cambridge
The Pitt Building, Trumpington Street, Cambridge CB2 1RP
40 West 20th Street, New York, NY 10011-4211, USA
10 Stamford Road, Oakleigh, Melbourne 3166, Australia

Women's work 1840–1940 first published by The Macmillan Press
Limited 1988
First Cambridge University Press edition 1995

Printed in Great Britain at the University Press, Cambridge

A catalogue record for this book is available from the British Library

Library of Congress cataloguing in publication data

Roberts, Elizabeth.
  Women's work 1840–1940 / prepared for the Economic History
Society by Elizabeth Roberts.
      p.   cm. – (New studies in economic and social history)
  First published in 1988.
  Includes bibliographical references and index.
  ISBN 0 521 55265 6 (hc). – ISBN 0 521 55788 7 (pb)
    1. Women – Employment – Great Britain – History. 2. Working class
women – Great Britain – History. I. Economic History Society. II. Title.
III. Series.
HD6135.R63   1995
331.4'0941–dc20   95–18418
                                                                 CIP

ISBN 0 521 55265 6 hardback
ISBN 0 521 55788 7 paperback

Contents

Acknowledgements

I should like to thank my colleague in the Centre for North-West Regional Studies, University of Lancaster, Mrs Marion McClintock, Dr Pat Thane of Goldsmiths' College, London, and Professor Leslie Clarkson of Queen's University for their support and helpful criticisms. Needless to say, I take full responsibility for any errors in the pamphlet and most notably for the many omissions which had to be made.

Note on references

References in the text within square brackets relate to the numbered items in the Bibliography, followed, where necessary, by the page numbers in italics, for example [1, 7–9].

Tables

1

Some general questions about women's work

This pamphlet attempts to survey women's work in Great Britain in the century 1840–1940. This first chapter raises some of the general questions, problems and characteristics of women's work in the period; the second examines in more detail women's paid full-time work; the third chapter looks at some of the social and economic aspects of married women's work both paid and unpaid; and the last chapter considers changes in women's working conditions and status and the roles of government, employers and unions.

It is probably over-ambitious to try to cover such an enormous topic in such a small space and the best that can be hoped is that questions will be raised and problems aired. Generalisations are inevitable as are aggregated data. These tend to obscure very important differences between areas and indeed between towns: it is hoped that the examples given will illuminate some of these individual differences. 1840 seems a reasonable time to begin. By then, the Industrial Revolution (whatever we may mean by that term) was well established and it was a time when public discussion of women's work was flourishing and the government was beginning to legislate directly about certain aspects of that work. Equally, 1940 seems a useful final date; the beginning of the Second World War and the commencement of a period which was to see very great changes in the lives and work of women.

In the century 1840–1940 there were significant and radical changes in many areas of British economic and social life: were there parallel changes in the world of women's work? One way of approaching the question of women's work in this period is to trace the continuing effects of industrialisation on the types of jobs done by women, or the number of women who worked for wages, the location of their work, their levels of skill and their degree of subordination to men (although it must be stressed that industrialisation happened at different rates in different areas with different consequences) [95]. However, anyone seeking fundamental alterations in job opportunities and in the status of and remuneration for women's work will not find them in this period.

In a brief treatment of women's work an attempt to look at the work of all classes of women would lead to excessive superficiality, therefore that of working-class women is given priority. There are, of course, difficulties in defining 'working-class', but generally the term is used to cover women who worked with their hands, who were paid wages, not salaries, and who did not employ other people; also, and most importantly, the wives and daughters of men who fitted the above description.

A proposed description of men's work might raise certain expectations in the reader, who would assume that the account would be of full-time paid work, which took place outside the home. No such assumptions can be made by those examining women's work in the period 1840–1940. Some women did indeed work full-time for wages in a place outside their home such as a workshop, shop or factory, or on the land, while others worked full-time for wages in their own homes or in other people's; others worked part-time for wages, both at home and away; and finally, very large numbers worked full-time at home for no wages at all. Unfortunately, since this work has never been paid it is somehow assumed that it is not 'real' work at all and consequently has become devalued in the eyes of many men and women.

This question of what is 'real' work is very important in any consideration of women's work [18]. Some historians have developed the idea that it is impossible to study women's role in the labour market without considering their role in the family as housewives and mothers. Women had a reproductive rather than productive role and as this reproductive work was unpaid society regarded it as having no economic value. This perception was translated to the labour market and a gender hierarchy of labour developed whereby women's work was given a lower social and economic value than that of men [57]. The complex interconnections between women's role in the home and family on one hand

and in the labour market on the other have been discussed by Tilly and Scott in *Women, Work and Family* [95]. Without understanding these interconnections and their complexities any study of women's work in this period is sterile.

Many aspects of women's work were controversial throughout the period. Women, married and unmarried, had always worked: they had been, for example, spinners, dressmakers, embroiderers, straw-plait and lacemakers; they had undertaken immense amounts of housekeeping and child-rearing. These activities did not appear to arouse controversy, but the public appearance of wage-earning working women, resulting from industrialisation, in certain areas like Lancashire, West Yorkshire and the Potteries produced (and continued to produce) endless comment, usually hostile, from contemporaries. Working wives and mothers especially were often regarded as unnatural, immoral and inadequate homemakers and parents. Male potters, in 1845, fearing a loss of work because certain machines were looked after by women, wrote a petition full of apparent concern for women and their children:

To maidens, mothers and wives, we say machinery is your deadliest enemy. . . . It will destroy your natural claims to home and domestic duties and will immure you and your toiling little ones in overheated and dirty shops, there to weep and toil and pine and die. [24, 6]

A year earlier, Lord Shaftesbury, speaking in the House of Commons on the Ten Hours Bill (finally passed in 1847), lamented that factory women were becoming like the roughest and worst kind of men:

They meet together to drink, sing and smoke; they use, it is stated, the lowest, most brutal and most disgusting language imaginable. . . . What is the ground on which the woman says she will pay no attention to her domestic duties, nor give the obedience which is owing to her husband? Because on her devolves the labour which ought to fall to his share, and she throws out the taunt, 'If I have the labour, I will also have the amusement'. [41, 76–7]

These two quotations, which could be replicated by hundreds of similar ones, encapsulate many of the criticisms made about factory women, especially those with husbands: that is, they were neglecting their duties at home, they were independent, they were immoral, and they were taking men's work. It is difficult to prove or disprove these criticisms for the earlier part of the period but for the last fifty years of it, oral evidence indicates a very different picture [76].

Unmarried women were also attacked; for example, 'pit-brow' lasses who worked above ground sorting coal, were criticised for being rough and masculine. In certain areas (notably around Wigan) it was observed that they even wore fustian trousers! A delegate at the Miners' Union Conference in 1863 said that it was 'a most sickening sight to see girls and women who had been created and designed for a much nobler sphere of action, clad in man's attire on the pit banks. But it is a much sadder sight to see them day by day losing everything modest.' [50, *180–1*].

These criticisms arose out of contemporary assumptions about women's work and indeed about the inherent nature and functions of women themselves. There is considerable difficulty in writing about these assumptions which were not always clearly articulated, which were not universally shared and which were ambivalent and contradictory. Some nineteenth-century feminists, for example, believed that women had to make a choice between work on one hand and marriage and motherhood on the other. But they firmly supported a woman's right to work outside the home [59, 2].

It is clear that the upper- and middle-class critics of working-class women did not in fact disapprove of *work* as such: indeed, it was seen as the 'sole correction and just retribution for poverty' [1, 62]. Most objections seemed to arise around the matter of location and when women were seen working away from their proper sphere; that is, their own, or someone else's home.

Historians frequently refer to 'domestic ideology', and Catherine Hall has argued that it is possible to see the formation of this ideology in the period 1780–1830, when the industrial bourgeoisie was emerging as a result of the Industrial Revolution [32]. Hall admits that the ideas which developed at that time had already been formulated and promulgated by the Puritans in the seventeenth century. Whatever the origins of this ideology it can be seen to have affected, throughout the nineteenth and twentieth centuries, many (but not all) of the prevalent attitudes of women and their work. Initially observable in the bourgeoisie, it spread to sections of all classes, and to members of both sexes. Expressed very simply, this domestic ideology saw the world divided into two spheres, one for men and one for women. Men were to go out to work, make money and support their families, while women were to stay at home, creating a haven for themselves and their children and for their husbands to return to. Men were to be concerned with the public sphere of the labour market and money-making. Women were to be involved in the private sphere of the home, dependent on their husbands for financial support, and certainly not expected to earn on their own account. (Well-rehearsed and frequently quoted aphorisms developed from this basic domestic ideology; a woman's place was in the home; there was men's work and women's work; a man should be paid a living family wage so that there should be no necessity for his wife, or indeed his daughters to work.)

These ideas not only affected those from the middle and upper classes who criticised working-class women who worked outside their homes; they also had a bearing on the attitudes of many working-class men and the women themselves. The latter can consequently be seen to display very ambivalent attitudes to their own work. Working-class women found themselves in a difficult position. Financially they were forced to work. Unmarried girls' wages were needed to supplement the family income.

There were large numbers of unmarried women with no pro- spect of being married. The 1881 census showed that there were one million more women than men and obviously large numbers of them had to earn their own living. Often married women could not manage on their husbands' earnings and as they frequently said, they worked because they had to. But many were not ashamed of this work; rather they were proud, believing that they were supporting and helping their families by working outside the home. They saw paid work, not as an alternative to housework, but as a way of enabling them better to fulfil their duty as wives, mothers and homemakers.

However, in general working-class women did *not* regard full time paid work as something they would undertake for the whole of their adult lives. Despite the demographical evidence about 'surplus' women, girls were often unwilling to serve apprentice- ships because they wanted the maximum wage possible between leaving school and leaving work when married. As Edward Cadbury observed in 1909 'few women expect to be life workers.

Practically all look forward to marriage as an escape from work'
[22, *138*].

Married women who were compelled to work for financial
reasons rarely continued to work when the financial crisis had
passed and it was assumed that their husbands would again keep
them. It may seem strange to modern readers that women as
recently as the 1930s (or indeed later) genuinely saw their emancipation as being a move *away* from paid work outside the home
towards staying there. It is perhaps more comprehensible when the
strength of the domestic idyll is appreciated and the nature of the
double burden of work carried by full-time working women is
understood [76]. It is difficult to ignore working-class women's
devotion to their families' need rather than their own. Indeed it is
doubtful if they perceived any conflict between the two [76]. In the
words of Jane Lewis: 'One point is clear, married women continued to believe firmly that their primary commitment was to
home and family' [59, *4*]. Some time earlier she also argued, 'it is
doubtful how far the majority of unskilled women workers have
ever moved away from the ideal of working for the family economy
and towards a more individualistic notion of working for their own
satisfaction' [58, *173*]. This is rather in contrast to the argument
advanced by Tilly and Scott [95].

Important as it is to understand this widely accepted ideology, it
is equally important to understand the very considerable poverty
experienced by so many working-class families in this period. This
poverty has been very well described, if not always quantified [26;
61; 72; 82; 88]. Poverty drove many women to wage-earning work
and it was widespread poverty which to some extent helps to
explain men's defensive attitude against women working. E. H.
Hunt wrote of the period 1850–1914:

Men believed that a limited amount of work was available and suspected
that allowing women to share work would cause some families to be
without pay as a consequence of other families taking more than their fair
share. [47, *24*]

Just as contemporaries held various assumptions about women's
work, so have historians of the period under discussion. They, too,
have been influenced by the 'domestic ideology' and have perhaps
based their analysis of women and their role and their work too

firmly on the assumption of a real separation of and differentiation between the public and private spheres. They write persuasively of the novel separation of 'home' and 'work' with industrialisation. Historians of working-class women would do well to examine what it was the women expended their effort on. For them there could be no clear distinction between the public and private spheres, however much ideally they would have liked there to be one. Married women who sold food from their back kitchens or front parlours nicely illustrate the merging of the public and private spheres which existed in so many women's lives. The confusion between public and private spheres is also well shown by the lives of those women taking in lodgers [23]. Some landladies operated quite formal businesses in their own homes, charging lodgers for their room, food, washing, and so on. But oral evidence also reveals that the most usual kind of lodger was in fact a relative who might or might not, depending on age, health and job, have paid for the lodgings [76]. It is thus particularly difficult to categorise landladies as belonging to, and working in, either the private or the public sphere. Most importantly of all, the typical working-class female job, throughout the period, was domestic service. Industrialisation, for the majority of women, did not separate work from the home; for domestic servants, and indeed for housewives, work continued to be done in a home and not in a factory. It can even be argued that industrialisation, by creating more wealth for the middle classes, indirectly resulted in more women working as domestic servants in expanding middle- and upper-class households [5].

Historians looking at women's work have understandably attempted to indicate how many women were involved in different occupations at various times. On these calculations can be based generalisations about the extent to which women were involved in the labour market (their participation rate) and about changing patterns of employment. There are, however, quite serious problems in attempting to use the data from census returns. Firstly there are very considerable difficulties in interpreting the data, as can be seen when studying secondary sources, and secondly there are doubts among historians about the accuracy of the evidence, especially for the nineteenth century. A small example will illustrate the first point. My own calculation of the total of domestic servants in Great Britain in 1851 is 1,224,419 (made by adding together the figures for England, Wales and Scotland). This includes domestic general servants, housekeepers, cooks, housemaids, nurses, inn-servants, charwomen, washerwomen and farm servants (indoors). It excludes nurses who were not domestic servants. Patricia Hollis gives a total of 1,135,000 [41], while Hunt suggests 1,027,000, but some of the difference here *might* be accounted for by his including only servants aged over 15 [47]. Burnett gives a figure of 751,641 but his is only for England and Wales [20]; the relevant figure for Scotland is 154,554, which still makes a much smaller final total than 1,224,419. The explanation of this discrepancy would appear to depend very much on who is defined as working in the capacity of domestic servant. (The census total for the whole of Great Britain is 1,234,212, which is different from the combined figures of England, Wales and Scotland. Could the difference be in the islands of the British seas?)

How reliable are the census data? There is an increasing awareness among historians that mistakes were made either by the original enumerators or by the householder or by both. (The enumerators' books are the documents on which the details of every household were recorded by the enumerator. This information was amalgamated into the published census returns. The enumerators' books are only open to inspection 100 years after their collection.) Edward Higgs, having looked at the data on the census enumerator's book for Rochdale and Rutland, suggests that the aggregated returns exaggerate the number of domestic servants. He argues that many 'domestic servants' enumerated as living with their extended families were not servants in the accepted sense of the word but either relatives helping out where, for example, the mother of the family was dead or where they were in fact acting as the female head of the house. Some enumerators appear to have used interchangeably the words 'housekeeper' and 'housewife' [37, 38]. There are various other definitional problems concerned with enumerating domestic servants. Farm servants (indoors), for example, undoubtedly also spent some of their time doing farm as opposed to domestic work; should they therefore be classed as agricultural workers? Again, domestic servants in retailing families unquestionably helped out in the shop, and were they therefore shop assistants?

Table 1.1 *Examples of differences between wage books and census returns*

Town and date		No. of women checked from wage books	No. and percentage of such women workers recorded with no occupation in the census returns	
			(No.)	(%)
Penicuik	1851	26	12	46
Galashiels	1851	8	8	100
Walkerburn	1861	6	6	100
Walkerburn	1881	6	5	83

(The author is grateful to Professor Michael Anderson for drawing this information to her attention and for Professor John Holley's permission to use it.)

There are more serious difficulties with the census returns which historians now recognise. It seems very likely that part-time work (usually undertaken by married women) was grossly underenumerated. One reason for this was that part-time work was so often casual and seasonal (for example fruit- and hop-picking which never took place at the same time as the census). It has been suggested that more part-time jobs might have been enumerated more often had householders been asked about work rather than about occupation. Returns were, however, undoubtedly influenced by the widespread assumption that married women were 'housewives'.

More surprising than the omission of married women's part-time work from the census, was the failure on occasions to count even their full-time work. Admittedly the evidence for these mistakes is still sparse but it is of great interest. Comparisons of wage books with workers' names and addresses, and census enumerators' books, for identical days, demonstrate that married women's full-time work was seriously underestimated. John Holley has examined the wage books of woollen mills in the Border region, checking the names and addresses of married women employees with the data in the enumerators' books. His findings raise disturbing questions for those using census data for a study of women's employment. Such data will be used in this book and obviously will continue to be used in similar historical work. They probably indicate trends adequately but exact figures and precise comparisons between years should be treated with very considerable caution. Some historians might well argue that census figures do not even indicate trends reliably. It is likely, for example, that the apparent downward trend in the number of domestic servants at the end of the nineteenth century is an effect of more accurate enumeration, especially of a more careful distinction between paid and unpaid labour [37; 38].

Did the percentage of women involved in the workforce increase, remain static or decline, both before and during the period 1840–1940? Historians writing about the Industrial Revolution are sometimes divided into two groups: the optimists and the pessimists. The 'optimistic' view argues that the Industrial Revolution gave women more job opportunities and led eventually to their emancipation [74]. R. M. Hartwell was especially enthusiastic:

It was during the Industrial Revolution, and largely because of the economic opportunities it afforded to working-class women, that there was the beginnings of that most important and most beneficial of all social revolutions of the last two centuries, the emancipation of women. [35, *343*]

The 'pessimistic' group of historians and observers at the time are less enthusiastic about the results of industrialisation but are divided as to its effects on women's participation rates in the labour market and on their status as workers.

Contemporaries who held what has come to be called the 'prelapsarian' view argue that labour in the pre-industrial world was creative, satisfying and wholesome. The opinions of John Ruskin and William Morris fall into this category [63]. Historians, taking a less romantic view, have suggested that home and work were more integrated and men and women more equal in pre-industrial times [95]. Other 'pessimists' consider that industrialisation, although producing more jobs for women, had a disastrous effect on the women, their homes, and their families. Such disparate voices as Friedrich Engels and Lord Shaftesbury shared this view. Still other writers in the pessimistic school agree that more women worked but believe that this was because of their

Table 1.2 *Female participation rates 1871–1931 (the percentage of females of all ages in 'occupations')*

Year	England & Wales (%)	Scotland (%)
1871	31	28
1891	27	27
	35[a]	
1911	26	24
	32[b]	
1931	27	
	34[c]	

[a] Of those aged over 10.
[b] Of those aged over 10.
[c] Of those aged over 14.

families' great poverty (an argument familiar to oral historians: women worked because they had to, not because of any motives of emancipation).

On the other hand, there are historians who suggest that women lost jobs because of industrialisation. Admittedly there were the new employments such as weaving, carding, and so on in the cotton mills, but women in other spheres such as home spinning entirely lost their trades. It is also argued that most of the new jobs resulting from industrialisation (as in iron- and steel-making and railway building) offered no employment at all to women. These writers tend to ignore the new service jobs which developed as a result of increasing prosperity among the bourgeoisie. More dressmakers, tailoresses and domestic servants, for example, were needed.

It is probable that we can never be certain about eighteenth- and nineteenth-century participation rates for women. This is partly because reliable eighteenth-century statistics do not exist and also because of the difficulties already referred to of using nineteenth-century census data. Eric Richards takes a rather extreme view by arguing that before the Industrial Revolution there was substantial female participation and that subsequently, as a result of industrial-

isation, female participation rates fell [75]. Hunt takes a more
balanced view:

The proportion of women at work in nineteenth-century Britain was
probably not larger than the proportion that had worked before the
Industrial Revolution. [47, *17*]

Michael Kelly in his introduction to Tilly and Scott's work wrote:
'Their book should bury effectively the notion that industrialisation
brought about the participation of a larger proportion of women in
the workforce' [95]. Tilly and Scott also argue that there are clear
continuities in women's work prior to and during the development
of industrial capitalism [95]. Indeed, as has already been suggested, to debate women's employment solely with reference to
industrialisation is a distortion of history. Even as late as 1861 only
about 30 per cent of the *whole* labour force was employed in the
new industries particularly associated with the Industrial Revolution [27, *109*]. To look solely at these industries ignores the work
done by the great majority of the population, especially the
women, who continued to work principally in their homes or small
workshops and not in factories.

After 1851 female participation rates can be calculated from the
censuses but the problems of enumeration must always be borne in
mind, and the figures should be regarded only as a very approx-
imate guide. Because of the nature of this pamphlet it has not been
felt appropriate to include a mass of statistics, therefore census
returns are given for 20-year intervals so that general trends can be
observed. As the reader will see, two sets of figures are given for
1891, 1911 and 1931. This is because of the introduction of
compulsory schooling after 1876. It was thought useful to include
the percentage of all ages in work so that comparisons could be
made throughout the period, and also percentages of those legally
entitled to work who actually did so.

Throughout the period the combined processes of industrialisation and urbanisation appear to have had little impact on women's
participation rates although again it must be emphasised that these
figures hide much unenumerated work. It is only in the period
after the Second World War that we see major changes in women's
employment. Hakim gives the participation rates for 1951, 1961

and 1971 as 45, 47 and 55 per cent [31] and Breugel cites 62 per cent for 1978 [18].

Reference has already been made to the 'domestic idyll'. This appears to have had a significant effect on the rates of return of women to work after child-bearing. Once women left full-time work, they rarely returned unless they were widowed or deserted. This is suggested in oral testimony and is borne out by statistical evidence about the ages of women at work. Hakim records that for 1901, 77 per cent of women in the age group 15–34 were at work but only 13 per cent were at work in the next group, 35–44, and only 11 per cent of those aged 45–59. The relevant figures for 1971 were 44 per cent of those aged 15–34, 21 per cent of those aged 35–44 and 55 per cent of those aged 45–59 [31]. The figures for 1901 reflect the pattern of women leaving work when they could afford to; those for 1971 reflect a new, post-Second World War trend of women who returned to work when their children were grown [18].

The pattern of the typical woman worker in full-time, wage-earning work as a young rather than an older person undoubtedly had some effect on the generally lower wages women earned compared to those of men [14]. In many industries (but not all) older, more experienced, workers could expect to earn higher wages. Obviously there were far fewer older women in work who might have 'boosted' the average wages for all women. However, aggregated figures should not be allowed to obscure the fact that sometimes women did earn more than men. In the cotton industry oral evidence has revealed many examples of individual highly skilled women weavers earning more than their male colleagues. The same was true in the Potteries, a very important area for female employment. Low aggregated wage rates hide the fact that highly skilled women decorators (doing transferring, gilding and painting) were paid more than some of the male potters doing less skilled jobs.

Differences within the age structures of male and female workers were not the only reason for different aggregated wage rates. (This important question will be examined further in Chapter 4.) There were widespread assumptions held about the relative value of men's work and women's work. Reference has already been made to the way a woman's status in the labour market tended to be defined by her familial role.

Many men argued that they had greater physical strength than women and were more skilled; therefore they deserved higher wages than women. In some cases these assumptions appear to have been based on gender stereotyping rather than on reality. Women expended prodigious amounts of strength and energy in, for example, the mining industry, in agriculture and in domestic work. Yet, on the other hand, women weavers in both the cotton and woollen textile industries explained the absence of female overlookers by the fact that women were not strong enough to lift the finished 'beam' of fabric out of the loom [14; 79]. Women textile workers also believed that they were not strong enough to 'walk' a spinning mule.

Women were often skilled (see above). But it is also true that throughout the period women were concentrated in unskilled jobs. One reason for this would appear to be a definite policy by male employers and male workers to 'deskill' work done by women. This can clearly be seen during the First World War (see Chapter 4). In the nineteenth century women home knitters taken into the Leicestershire hosiery factories were divested of their previously recognised skills and given unskilled tasks and were assured of low wages and status [70]. Industrialisation in some industries (especially the sweated trades) came to mean extensive subdivision of the labour process and men fearful of losing skilled jobs and good wages insisted on women taking the less skilled, low-status jobs [51, *10*]. Charles More in *Skill and the English Working Class* has very little to say about women workers (they do not appear in his index). He writes:

Women have not been considered because it is not possible to fit women's work in to the general hypothesis of skill and its acquisition advanced here. This is because women were excluded by custom not merely from apprenticed trades but from practically every occupation which led to the acquisition of skill. Excluded from these apprenticeships, women formed a vast pool of necessary unskilled labour which was usually paid less than the minimum wage of an unskilled male. [66, *229*]

He does not define 'custom' or suggest who made it, and ignores the skills of, for example, weavers, dressmakers and milliners. Snell argues that the loss of skilled occupations by women in the nineteenth century was part of a process which started in the seventeenth century when women had worked in many artisan trades. Women progressively lost both apprenticeships and skilled work. He suggests that the sexual division of labour became stronger with the advance of industrialisation [85, *ch. 6*].

The ideal of a family wage whereby a male worker could support his family without his wife having to work was widely supported (and is still far from uncommon). The implication of a man receiving a family wage was that women should not do so as they did not support a family. Indeed in law, marriage and ideology, women were deemed to be dependants [55].

This attitude ignored the plight of widowed and deserted women and of single women supporting elderly relatives. The question of a family wage has been a source of endless debate and controversy both historically and among contemporary historians. Eric Hobsbawm has argued that few married women were in paid employment and that the pattern of male breadwinner and dependent wife was not simply an ideal but a fact of life [14]. Feminist historians would argue that married women often had to work because of the inadequacy of their husbands' wage [76; 78; 14]. This is not to say that most working-class women did not accept that in an ideal world men should still be the family breadwinners [59, *181*]. There was, not unsurprisingly, widespread support among women for the concept of the family wage (see Chapter 4). Jane Humphries has argued that this was not a sexist device adopted by nineteenth-century working-class men but a strategy adopted by both men and women against exploitation by the capitalist system. She maintains that without the family wage all wage levels would have fallen, forcing men and women members of the family to work. Continued flooding of the labour market would in turn force down wages. By restricting the labour market mostly to men and by holding up men's wages this form of exploitation was restricted [46]. On the other hand, Heidi Hartman sees the concept of the family wage coming directly from men's determination to maintain their privileges over women [34]. A direct criticism of Jane Humphries' views was made by Michelle Barratt and Mary McIntosh, who argued that the concept of a family wage enforced the dependency and oppression of women, reduced single, divorced and widowed women into dire poverty and divided the working classes [6].

Table 1.3 *Average earnings of females as a percentage of those for males in selected industrial groups, 1906–35*

Groups	1906	1924	1931	1935
Textiles	58.5	56.1	56.0	55.9
Clothing	46.3	49.1	50.2	51.2
Food, drink, tobacco	41.5	48.1	48.7	47.0
Paper, printing	36.4	39.6	39.4	37.3
Metal industries	38.1	44.7	47.6	45.7
Total (all industries)	43.7	47.7	48.3	48.0

Sources: [58; 16].

Some women feared the granting of equal wages for equal work because they thought it would lead to an employer automatically employing male workers. A Miss Whyte of the London Bookbinders made this complaint to the Trades Union Congress in 1900:

As to the statement of the Trade Unions that they were willing to admit women, as long as they received equal pay with men, the women knew that such a rule would operate to the entire exclusion of women for if a woman offered herself in competition with a man for the same work the latter would be accepted. [64, *102*]

This apparent low self-evaluation of women, their skills and their work is a continuing theme of this period. And yet Miss Whyte may well have been talking sense, especially with reference to the printing industry.

Whatever the reasons, women's average wages remained low compared to those of men well beyond the end of the period. Hollis wrote: 'It was the coming of full employment in the twentieth century that was to transform men's wage rates. Women had to wait until the legislation of the 1970s' [41, *54*]. As long ago as 1902 Clara Collett wrote: 'There is no hardship in women working for a living, the hardship lies in not getting a living when they work for it' [51, *30*].

Some historians would, and do, argue that any evaluation of equal pay for equal work is somewhat misleading because of the segregation of work between men and women:

Occupational segregation on the basis of sex exists where men and women do different kinds of work so that one can speak of two separate labour forces, one male and one female which are not in competition with each other for the same jobs. [31, *1*]

There are numerous examples of occupational segregation. There were many occupations where no women were found at all; the 1911 census reveals no women in the army or navy, or as priests, ministers, engineers, surveyors, railway engine drivers, guards, riveters, plasterers, fitters and turners, blast furnace workers or dock labourers. There were, of course, no women in Parliament. The list is selective and could be considerably lengthened if extended to include jobs in which very few women were employed. Although there were jobs reserved exclusively, or almost exclusively, for men, it is more difficult to make a list of occupations kept solely for women. The only four traceable from the 1911 census were nuns, midwives, day girls (servants) and charwomen. (There were, however, many male indoor servants working in different capacities: 42,034 in fact.)

All other work done by women was shared with men and here it becomes difficult to use the concept of occupational segregation with its notion of two labour markets. It was in these areas where so many problems about wages and status arose, with men and women apparently competing for the same or nearly similar jobs. In 1911 there were 12,960 men and 18,449 women bookbinders; 82,341 men and 190,927 women cotton weavers; 20,486 men and 59,171 women cotton winders and warpers; 122,352 men and 127,115 women tailors; there were also 40,434 men and 29,439 women engaged in the manufacture of earthenware, china and porcelain.

Finally, there were considerable geographical variations both in patterns of work and in wages. Regional wage variations are discussed by E. H. Hunt [48]. It will be clear already from Table 1.2 that Scotland had proportionately fewer women in full-time paid work than there were in England. There were great regional variations in the percentage of married women at work, as will be seen in Chapter 3. These variations depended to a large extent on the local labour market and what jobs were available. To state the obvious, women had little chance of being weavers in Dorset or pottery workers on Tyneside. But there were other reasons for local variations resulting from local traditions and assumptions. Women, for example, did not generally work in the Northumberland and Durham coalfield whereas their employment as pitbrow lasses was common in the Lancashire coalfield [50]. Conversely, brick-making was a woman's trade in the Black Country but in Lancashire it was a male preserve. (This was possibly because in the Black Country men had alternative work in the iron works, whereas in Lancashire women had alternative work in the mills.) In the 1880s astonished East Anglians watched the wives and daughters of migrant Scots farmers doing jobs that in East Anglia were thought of as exclusively men's work [47].

All the factors affecting women's work described in this chapter came together in varying combinations in separate geographical areas and in different occupations. Thus the status of the woman worker and her own view of her role were not uniform throughout the United Kingdom. Tilly and Scott [95] effectively challenged those who argued that women were 'modernising' at the same time and pace throughout the country. It is essential to bear this qualification in mind when reading a book of this brevity. All generalisations about women's work and women workers need considerable qualification. Moreover the pattern of women's work and its problems will become more complex as local studies continue to be made.

2

Women's full-time paid employment

(i) Domestic servants

Despite the great growth in the textile industries, the most common occupation for working-class girls and women throughout the period was domestic service. It has been pointed out that making the material for a shirt occupied a Lancashire weaver for about thirty minutes but its subsequent life required about twelve hours of washing, starching and ironing [47, *19*]. Despite their large numbers domestic servants were overlooked by historians until comparatively recently [20; 37; 38; 39; 42; 62]. The reasons for this neglect are manifold. Domestic servants had no trade union, they took little part in class or political struggle, they were mostly female, they themselves regarded their work as temporary, they were hidden away in private homes rather than prominently displayed in factories, and they performed services which had no 'exchange' value. They therefore do not show up readily in contemporary documentation.

Table 2.1 *Domestic servants (all ages)*

Date	Total (England and Wales)	% of total female population	Total (Scotland)	% of total female population
1851	1,069,865	9.8	154,554	10.2
1871	1,508,888	12.8	155,307	8.9
1891	1,759,555	11.6	190,051	9.1
1911	1,662,511	11.1	159,658	6.5
1931	1,600,017	7.7	170,544	6.8

Some of the difficulties in enumerating domestic servants have been described in Chapter 1, and the categories mentioned from the 1851 census have been used as far as possible. But, as with many other occupations, these census categories change not only their name but also their function. In 1871 laundry workers replace washerwomen in the census data. They continue to be included here in the enumeration of domestic servants but the problem of this approach must be acknowledged. Laundry workers obviously could and did include washerwomen but the category, by the end of the century, included those working in large commercial laundries, who could perhaps be more accurately described as factory workers.

With these many reservations it is possible to see both an initial increase (1851–71) and then a decline in percentages of girls and women employed as domestic servants in the period (and most especially after the First World War in England and Wales; although as has already been stated this could be the result of changes in enumeration). The overall decline in actual numbers of domestic servants was not, however, dramatic and the total remained considerable.

Generalisations are difficult about such a large group of workers, but most observers (as opposed to some employers) agreed that the women worked very hard. It was calculated in 1873 that a housemaid's day extended from 6 a.m. to 10 p.m., during which time she had two half-hours for meals and an hour and a half 'break' for needlework in the afternoon. This meant 12 hours actual work, which was two hours longer than that of factory women [20]. There was little technology in the home and so cleaning and cooking required a vast amount of physical effort.

It has been frequently stated that domestic servants were usually country girls who had very few alternative forms of employment, and also suggested that they would accept living and working conditions which were unacceptable to their more sophisticated town cousins. Certainly many country girls can be found among the ranks of domestic servants but so too can many from the town. In towns where heavy industries (iron and steel, shipbuilding, engineering) predominated there were often few job opportunities for girls other than domestic service. Oral evidence shows that many girls either found situations as domestic servants locally or, like their country counterparts, travelled quite considerable distances for work. (This out-migration of girls and women as domestic servants is one of the features which caused an excess of males in some towns with heavy industries, like for example, Barrow-in-Furness.)

The vast majority of domestic servants had in common a heavy work load but they did not all share the same social status. There were obvious and important differences between being a day girl in a small suburban household and the cook in 10 Downing Street, and all servants were affected by the social status of their employers. Within a household there were also considerable differences in the power and influence of, for example, the housekeeper or the kitchen maid, and there were also male and female status hierarchies involved. Each servant (except in single-servant households) had different duties, wages and privileges and accepted their place in the domestic hierarchy. A perusal of a household manual of the time will illustrate some of the complexities and indeed peculiarities of the system (the most famous of these, by Mrs Beeton, first appeared in 1861 and was republished throughout the period).

Domestic servants themselves by the beginning of the twentieth century displayed a certain ambivalence towards questions of status arising from their occupation. Women who had been domestic servants sometimes, after marriage, translated (as far as was possible) the habits and standards they had learned into their own life style. An underlying assumption that these ways were somehow better than those of their neighbours is discernible. Oral evidence shows women emphasising the importance of correct table settings and correct table manners; one family had the lodgers eating at a separate table. There are examples of women believing that their experience in domestic service improved both their own and their families' status. Edward Higgs, however, argues that being a domestic servant was more likely to cause downward rather than upward social mobility [39]. Interestingly, women who had been domestic servants did not send their own daughters into domestic service; they wanted something 'better' for them, for example, shop-work [76].

Certainly by the end of the nineteenth century there were increasing complaints from members of the middle and upper classes about the shortage of servants. Ironically this could no longer be ascribed to the low wages earned by these workers. Many attempts have been made to calculate the average wages for domestic servants [20; 39]. It is clear from various sources (for example advertisements in newspapers) that wages rose throughout the second half of the nineteenth century. The wages still appeared to be very low, however. Average annual wages (taken from advertisements in *The Times*) for 1907 were £19 10s for general servants and £26 8s for parlourmaids. What is difficult to compute is the monetary value of the board, lodgings and uniform provided by the employer. In a 'good' household where everything was provided and was of a satisfactory standard, it could be argued that the maid's wages were in fact pocket money and that for those days she had a reasonable disposable income out of which it was possible to save. Theresa McBride argues that domestic servants (not just in Great Britain but in France and the USA as well) had a distinct wage advantage over other female workers [62, *119*].

However, the noticeable rise in wages which was presumably forced on employers by 'the servant shortage' did not solve the shortage. An increasing number of women regarded the wages as insufficient compensation for what were regarded as the inherent problems of domestic service: the long hours; the hard physical effort; being at someone's 'beck and call'; the lack of independence and the frequent loneliness of women in small, single-servant households. It is clear that when alternative employment became available women tended to choose that in preference to domestic work.

Pamela Horn connects the decline of the Victorian servant to the increase in alternative employment [42]. Higgs argues, however, that while town girls preferred, whenever possible, to have alternative occupations to domestic service, for country girls it continued to represent an easily available and acceptable occupation. He also argues that the difficulty in finding servants experienced towards the end of the nineteenth century was because of the decline in the rural population [39].

It must be stressed that for many women domestic work remained their only available occupation and domestic servants remained the largest female occupational group throughout the period.

Table 2.2 *Female textile workers in different materials*

Date	Cotton		Woollens & worsteds		Silk		Flax		Jute & hemp	
	E & W	S	E & W	S	E & W	S	E & W	S	E & W	S
1851	247,705	26,675	96,638	6,641	68,342	1,059	13,219	39,579	4,818	1,816
1871	279,870	13,188	117,494	14,117	51,100	1,256	10,629	26,863	1,516	3,677
1891	332,784	11,909	130,094	18,123	31,811	2,615	5,592	19,216	2,333	22,059
1911	374,785	9,360	127,148	15,148	29,643	810	2,930	16,360	995	27,074

Unfortunately the 1931 census aggregated figures group all textile workers together.

E & W = England and Wales

S = Scotland

(ii) Textile workers

It is often assumed that the Industrial Revolution transformed the manufacture of textiles, moving it from the home to the factory and introducing machine instead of hand power. By and large this transformation had taken place by 1840 but the process was not complete. Some cotton handloom weavers (always men) remained working until the 1850s, silk handloom weaving at home continued well into the twentieth century and the handloom weaving of woollens continues in the Highlands and Islands of Scotland to this day.

Table 2.2 shows the number of women workers working with each textile material throughout the period and there are many obvious trends; the great expansion of the cotton industry in England until 1911 and indeed until the end of the First World War. This expansion was accompanied by the steady decline of the Scottish cotton industry as it became more and more concentrated in Lancashire. The manufacture of woollens and worsteds continued to expand both in West Yorkshire and in the Border region of Scotland until the turn of the century when both industries began to suffer a decline. The flax industry (i.e. the manufacture of linen) continued to decline in England, Wales and Scotland, as did the silk industry. The jute industry (concentrated on Dundee) expanded and flourished in Scotland (and for a brief time in England, so much so that a jute mill existed in Barrow-in-Furness until a series of fires in the 1890s brought its life more or less to an end).

The sharp decline in the number of textile workers between 1911 and 1931 is mostly accounted for by the slump in the cotton industry following the First World War. Because of the dominant position of the cotton industry in British textiles, the emphasis

Table 2.3 *Total number of female textile workers*

	England and Wales	Scotland
1851	430,722	75,770
1871	460,009	59,101
1891	502,614	73,922
1911	535,501	68,752
1931	330,700	42,989

Table 2.4 *Percentages of women textile workers in different materials: 1851 and 1911*

	England and Wales (%)	Scotland (%)
1851		
Cotton	57	35
Hemp	1	2
Silk	16	1
Woollens	22	9
Flax	3	52
1911		
Cotton	69	14
Silk	5	2
Flax	0.5	24
Woollens	23	22
Hemp and jute	0.2	39

within textiles inevitably focuses on that single theme, and indeed the rest of this section is concerned with women in the cotton industry. However, Table 2.4 is included to illustrate the different relative significance of various textile materials in England and Wales compared with Scotland at two different dates.

In the Lancashire cotton industry women had more equality with men than in most other industries. Women were combers, carders, warpers and weavers and, as new machines were introduced, ring spinners. The only major process from which they were excluded was mule spinning. Male mule spinners resolutely refused to admit women to their craft. Women were also excluded from being tacklers or overlookers (the person in charge of a group of weavers). No trace has been found of a female in such a position, and when women weavers are asked about this they usually say that overlookers had to carry the beams (the warp threads wound onto a large roller), fit them to the looms and then later remove the full beams. They were carried across the shoulders and women weavers always say this feat was beyond their physical strength (see Chapter 1). On the other hand, most women weavers claimed to be as technically competent (if not more so) than the tackler when it came to mending (or 'fettling') the looms and it is likely that their ability to balance weights could have become as accomplished as their male colleagues if they had had the opportunity.

Women weavers were well paid compared with most other women workers. Oral evidence also reveals that they could and did earn more than unskilled men in other areas of employment and a good woman worker could earn as much and more than a male weaver: wages were paid by the piece, and piece rates were the same for men and women. However, much depended on the policy of each mill's management. It is clear (see Table 1.3) that, using aggregated figures, women weavers were earning less than men. There were various reasons offered for this, such as that men weavers operated more looms – in 1937, 26 per cent of men but only 14 per cent of women operated six looms instead of four. (No one in Preston, male or female, remembered any six-loom operatives until after the Second World War.) Some factory managements, presumably influenced by concepts of a family wage for men, offered men the better priced cloth and gave them work in preference to the women when beams were scarce, and it is also suggested that men worked longer hours than women [81]. The age disparity between men and women (see p. 13) also accounted for the wage gap in cotton weaving. Even given these explanations, however, wage differentials were less marked than in other industries (see Chapter 1).

(iii)   Shop-keeping and shop-work

There are major problems in attempting to enumerate accurately the number of women employed in shop-work. As will be seen in Chapter 3, very many married women were involved in some form of trading, often on a temporary, part-time or casual basis. Wives of shopkeepers who worked very hard in the shop, but probably on a less than full-time basis, were excluded from the census in 1881. There is also the problem of distinguishing between shop assistants and shopowners and managers, since they all appear, before the First World War, under the general heading of 'dealers'. Moreover this category, in the earlier part of the period, undoubtedly included women who *made* goods. The

1851 census enumerates such groups as dealers, workers in leather, other dealers, workers in silk. By 1911 makers and dealers are distinct but any comparisons between 1851 and 1911 are more or less impossible.

There is also the difficulty of ascertaining the class origin of these dealers; undoubtedly some were working-class but many must have been prosperous members of the bourgeoisie. It is clear from oral evidence that shopkeepers came from a very wide range of social backgrounds, enjoyed different social status and had very variable levels of financial success. However great the problems of enumeration are, historians and contemporary observers alike are agreed that there was much expansion in shop work and that by 1931 shops provided a major source of employment for women [28; 40]. The 1931 census for England and Wales enumerated 544,121 women involved in shop-work; 149,590 owners and managers, and 394,531 shop assistants.

For many working-class families working in a shop carried more social status than working either in a factory or in domestic service. Most shop-work was not as physically demanding as that in the other two occupations, but conditions and wages were frequently poor. Young girls working in large department stores were, in some cases, obliged to live in huge and often uncomfortable dormitories [11]. This arrangement was ended by the Shop Hours Act of 1906 but the working day continued to be very long. A survey published in 1910 suggested that girls in 'first-class' shops could expect a 60–65 hour week but those in less 'classy' shops could work up to 85 hours per week, as compared with $55\frac{1}{2}$ hours per week in pre-1914 factories.

An Act of 1913 established that shop-workers should work 'only' 64 hours per week. It is clear from oral evidence, however, that shop girls, especially in small, owner-managed shops, often did 'voluntary' overtime. They appeared to make little protest; indeed Margaret Bondfield, and Mary MacArthur, two prominent women trade unionists, suggested that the 'genteel' nature of the shop assistants made them difficult to induct into any self-help organisations. Women shop assistants in many cases did identical work to men but their wages were not equivalent, and in 1900 women earned about 65 per cent of the average male wage.

(iv)   Clerical and office work

In 1914 about 20 per cent of clerical workers were women. Between 1861 and 1911 the number of male clerks had increased fivefold while the number of women clerks had risen by 400 per cent [40]. The expansion of large commercial firms and the growth of insurance, banking and communications all provided more jobs for women. The new skills of shorthand and typing were generally and perhaps illogically presumed to be peculiarly suitable for women. Some historians have suggested that employers engaged women in clerical and secretarial work because they expected women to be dutiful and compliant workers [40]. Meta Zimmeck, however, gives a picture of less than down-trodden women clerical workers [98]. More traditional employers continued to employ male clerks until the First World War, but as men went off to fight, it became imperative to engage women as clerical workers. Unlike the women who were taken on in the engineering and armaments industries (see Chapter 4) and who lost their jobs at the end of the war, women in clerical jobs were generally kept on, and their numbers continued to increase, as Table 2.5 shows.

Before the war few women clerks had been working-class, but after the war, as oral evidence indicates, more and more working-class girls, especially those from aspiring families, who had perhaps had an extra year at school, or who had been to the technical school or even to a grammar school, entered clerical occupations. This type of work certainly enjoyed more social status than any of the occupations described above and it was also comparatively well paid. Some clerks from the inter-war period mention wages of £2 a week, which was more than women earned in any of the other occupations available to working-class girls, and about the level of

Table 2.5 *Women clerical workers*

	1911 and 1931	
	England and Wales	Scotland
1911	149,215	33,567
1931	1,184,778	173,366

wages for an unskilled man. But clerical work had few opportunities for advancement and many employers operated a marriage bar by which women had to leave work at the time of marriage [98]. Yet the dramatic increase in the number of women in clerical jobs marks a major change in the pattern of women's employment in the period.

(v) Dressmakers, milliners, tailoresses

It is very difficult to gain any clear idea of how many people were involved in the making of clothes during this period. It is presumed that those women enumerated in the census as dressmakers, milliners or tailoresses were employed in workshops on a full-time basis. A lot of clothing was in fact produced by out-workers – i.e. women employed by someone else (see section vi) – and by women working independently on their own account as dressmakers at home (see Chapter 3), including those making clothes solely for their own use.

Dressmakers and milliners served a long and arduous apprenticeship, sometimes paying their employers for the privilege of working. The wages received were usually very small but a time-served dressmaker had learned some very useful skills, and an examination of pre-1914, handmade clothes in a museum will reveal the very considerable abilities of their makers. These skills stood a woman in good stead so that when she married, she could clothe her family and perhaps also set up a small home-centred business.

Tailoring was dominated by men who were determined to keep their trade out of the hands of women; as early as 1834 men tailors excluded women from their union [89]. Eventually, however, they were forced to admit women to the tailoring shops, for if costs were to be kept down, women, who could be paid less, had to be employed. The women, however, were not allowed to carry out such important jobs as cutting-out or making-up the garments, and their role tended to be confined to oversewing seams and making buttonholes. Like dressmakers, they continued to work very long hours and earn little money. One tailoress who made buttonholes reported her first wage, about 1930, was 15 shillings

Table 2.6 *Dressmakers, milliners and tailoresses*

	England and Wales	Scotland
1911	405,818	63,701
1931	280,383	30,565

(75p). (She was paid 1½d for a jacket buttonhole and 2d for one in an overcoat [76, *68*].)

Table 2.6 shows a drop in the number of dressmakers, milliners and tailoresses from 1911 to 1931. This was probably due to foreign competition and to competition from factory-produced clothes.

(vi)   Out-workers, homeworkers and the sweated trades

It is important to define what is meant by the terms 'sweated trade', 'out-workers' and 'homeworker' [67]. The word 'sweating' was used in the nineteenth and early twentieth centuries to condemn the conditions under which some people worked, namely for long hours for very low wages in frequently appalling conditions. Out-workers and homeworkers were not necessarily the same people. Out-work was the contracting out of tasks to a group of workers employed in a small factory or workshop. The out-workers often carried out a single process in the chain of production (such as pressing clothes) but sometimes they made a complete article (such as a matchbox). Homeworkers, as the name implies, worked at home on raw materials supplied by an employer. The homeworkers were the most exploited [67].

By the mid-nineteenth century, except in large cities like Manchester, Leeds, Sheffield and Newcastle, homework had disappeared from the North of England. In the Midlands, however, the pattern was very different: for example, in Birmingham many women made nails and chains in sheds attached to their houses; Nottingham women made lace and hosiery at home; Northampton women made boot and shoes. One of the largest concentrations of homeworkers was in London where women worked in the various garment trades. Mayhew in the 1850s described a waistcoat worker who might receive 6d, 8d or 10d a waistcoat, and who averaged about 3 shillings (15p) a week. She was forced to work from 9 a.m. to 11 p.m. to earn even that pittance, and often went hungry as a result. Morris quotes wages for homeworkers in the tailoring trade in 1906 [67]. For a working day of between 10 to 16 hours, they earned between 5 to 10 shillings (25–50p) a week (the only exception being those who made voile shirts). Not all London homeworkers necessarily worked in the garment trade. Clementina Black described women making matchboxes; they had to make 144 boxes for 2d [64, *113–14*].

Out-workers and homeworkers were predominantly women:

Of necessity the supply of outworkers was bound to consist largely of women and children, of grandparents, wives, unmarried and widowed sisters and daughters and young boys; and among these the female element predominated. [21, *195*]

Indeed Bythell goes further and argues that until the last quarter of the nineteenth century not only were most out-workers women, but most of the women who worked in industry did so as out-workers. It is virtually impossible to enumerate these workers: however, at the beginning of the twentieth century, local authorities were obliged by the Factory Acts to collect lists of out-workers' names from employers. The lists for 1907 produced 105,633 employees working at home, 86,000 of whom were making wearing apparel (the next largest group being 5363 lace-makers), and London had a third of the national total. Bythell regards this figure as incomplete and suggests that it should be multiplied by a factor of three or four.

There were out-workers attached to many industries, including some with a fair degree of mechanisation. These industries varied, depending on which part of the country is being examined. They included silk weaving, lacemaking, dressmaking and knitting, insewing of boots and shoes, straw-plaiting, and the making of boxes, brushes, artificial flowers and the carding of such items as buttons, hooks, eyes and pins and most particularly the tailoring trades in London and Leeds [67; 84]. In general stitching and seaming became the characteristic activities of the homeworkers.

It is probable that the number of homeworkers increased at

the end of the nineteenth and the beginning of the twentieth centuries. The Factory and Workshop Acts of 1891 and 1895 regulated working activities in sewing and tailoring workshops and it would seem likely that manufacturers, in order to keep down costs, subcontracted even more work to out-workers. Many critics of the out-work system believed it would be impossible to regulate working conditions in private homes. The difficulties are indeed obvious. However, there was some help for out-workers in the fixing of minimum wages from 1909 onwards (see Chapter 4).

Out-work did decline after 1909, but it is probable that cheap foreign imports had as much to do with the decrease as the fixing of minimum wages. The straw-plait industry declined markedly at the end of the nineteenth century in the face of cheap imports from China from 1873 onwards. Garment workers suffered similarly in the inter-war period. Out-work has, however, never entirely disappeared and examples of grossly exploited women homeworkers can still be found in the 1980s.

(vii)   Innkeepers, publicans, café proprietors, lodging house keepers

This is yet another group of women where a really accurate estimation of numbers is impossible. The problems of enumerating women who had lodgers have already been referred to in Chapter 1. Until 1881 the census not only counted innkeepers, beerhouse keepers and so on but also their wives. This was a sensible recognition that in the catering trade, with its myriad of small businesses, most wives would help their husbands in many crucial ways. After 1881 such women were not enumerated although common sense and oral evidence indicate that they worked as hard, and in some cases, harder than their husbands. Without further research, there is no apparent explanation for the fluctuation in numbers of women employed in these various branches of catering in Scotland and neither is it clear why there was such a marked decline in England and Wales after the First World War; problems of enumeration may well be the reason.

Table 2.7 *Innkeepers, publicans, lodging house keepers, café proprietors*

	England and Wales	Scotland
1851	30,220	7,098
1871	43,282	10,380
1891	77,884	6,008
1911	147,395	4,914
1931	109,952	6,149

(viii) Agriculture

Women had always been involved in agriculture. They had made butter and cheese, milked cows, fed chickens, helped with calving and lambing and with haymaking, harvest and fruitpicking. The decline in the number of women involved in agriculture reflects growing mechanisation but the decline may in practice have been less dramatic than might appear. There is, as always, the problem of farmers' wives and daughters, who helped out when needed but who are not enumerated as farm workers. And of course the census failed to count the many women who worked seasonally (see Chapter 1). The variety of the work they did and the severity of their lot, especially those who worked in gangs, is vividly portrayed by Jennie Kitteringham [52].

There were, however, great variations in women's agricultural work over time and space. From about 1750, for example, women in grain-producing areas found their work marginalised as the sickle, the tool they had used for harvesting, was increasingly replaced by the heavier scythe judged to be suitable for use only by men [44]. Snell advances this argument about women's declining role in agriculture by suggesting that between about 1750 and 1843 (the date of the report of the Employment of Women and Children in Agriculture) there had been a striking reduction in the number of agricultural jobs open to women [85, 52].

But women were not excluded from all heavier farm work: there were the notorious agricultural gangs (regulated by Act of Parliament in 1867). In the North of England women generally cut the harvest until well into the nineteenth century; in Northumberland,

Table 2.8 *Female agricultural workers (not farmers)*

	England and Wales	Scotland
1851	44,319	26,151
1871	33,513	22,174
1891	24,150	22,046
1911	13,214[a]	6,127

[a]These figures exclude market gardeners who were increasing in numbers by 1911.

where there were alternative jobs for men but few for women, women did very heavy farm work until the end of the nineteenth century [51].

3
Some social and economic aspects of the work of married women

The last chapter surveyed women's full-time work. Some full-time working women were married and it is a matter of observation that they tended to cluster in particular industries, for example, those producing china and porcelain, cotton and various items of clothing [51; 67; 70]. However, before the census of 1901 when aggregated tables of percentages of married women in work were given, it is not easy to estimate how many married women were in full-time work. Before 1901 they were listed in the census enumerators' books, although this may be an incomplete record; (see Chapter 1) but they do not appear in the aggregated tables.

There were wide geographical differences in the percentages of married women employed in full-time work as Table 3.1 illustrates. It will be noticed that towns where a relatively high percentage of married women worked also had a higher percentage of unmarried girls in work, thus reflecting the generally more favourable state of the local female labour market.

Married women who worked full-time incurred a great deal of criticism throughout the period (see Chapters 1 and 4). Mrs Bayley, in a report to the National Association for the Promotion of Social Science in 1861 wrote: 'the wife and mother going abroad for work is a fine example of a waste of time, a waste of property, a waste of morals and a waste of health and life and ought in every way to be prevented' [36, *1*]. The commentary on the census returns in 1911 boasted of married women that: 'The great bulk of women are fortunately, in this country, free at all ages to devote their attention to the care of their households' [47, *18*]. The implied criticism of those not staying at home is clear. The issue of married women in full-time work became particularly

Table 3.1 *Percentages of unmarried and married women in full-time work in 1911*

(a)	Unmarried (%)	Married (%)
England and Wales	54.5	13.7
Urban districts	56.8	14.8
Rural districts	45.8	9.3

(b) A sample of towns with over 20% of married and widowed women in full-time work in 1911

	Unmarried (%)	Married & widowed (%)
Blackburn	78.0	42.5
Burnley	76.6	40.0
City of London	77.3	42.3
Hinkley	75.0	41.2
Leek	73.7	34.8
Luton	68.2	36.7
Macclesfield	72.2	34.1
Nottingham	68.7	25.9
Preston	74.5	35.0
Stockport	68.6	24.4
Stoke-on-Trent	63.0	34.8
Todmorden	75.9	25.7

(c) A sample of towns and counties with less than 20% of married and widowed women in full-time work in 1911

	Unmarried (%)	Married & widowed (%)
Barrow-in-Furness	40.6	6.9
Cornwall	45.4	8.8
Durham (County)	29.9	5.3
Ebbw Vale	28.3	4.9
Lancaster	49.2	11.0
London	62.3	18.5
Maidenhead	60.0	15.8
Rotherham	35.2	6.6
Staffordshire	48.7	10.4
Sunderland	40.7	8.3
York	55.9	10.7
Yorkshire (West Riding)	55.2	11.4

acute after the end of the First World War, for although their work in transport, munitions, on the land and in offices and factories had played a major part in helping to win the war [17], there was a national campaign in the press and in Parliament to persuade, indeed force, the women back into the home. Most women did in fact bow to these pressures and returned to being solely house-wives. Some of them were affected by the notion of the domestic idyll (see Chapter 1). Others, with the increased prosperity enjoyed by those families where the fathers were in full-time employment, saw no need for their continuing to work [59, 3].

Yet poverty continued to drive many women to full-time paid work (see Chapter 1). As the Interdepartmental Committee on Physical Deterioration said in 1904 of wage-earning wives: 'The one wage was insufficient to keep the family in the standard of life they expect'. In the same year the principal lady factory inspector suggested the following reasons for married women working: firstly, the death of the father or the lack of employment or insufficiency of the father's wages; secondly, desertion by the father; and thirdly, a preference for the factory as opposed to the home. She concluded that the first reason was by far and away the most important. Much later in the century, in 1957, Viola Klein conducted a survey of married women in full-time work and concluded that 67 per cent of women from social class 'C' and 79 per cent from social classes 'D' and 'E' worked for financial reasons [53].

How in fact did a married woman's full-time work affect her role as wife and mother? How justified were the criticisms which were made of these women? How successful were they in their aim of improving their families' standard of living? In the widespread absence of letters, diaries or relevant books, much of the evidence about the interaction of a woman's work at home and in the factory comes from oral evidence. This, by its nature, refers specifically to the period after 1890, and even more specifically to women working in the cotton industry from whom the information was collected.

Full-time working mothers did not neglect their children. There was a well-organised, well-paid child-minding service provided by relatives and neighbours. Even the Preston Medical Officer of Health, whose predecessors had long castigated working mothers, agreed in 1930 that the children were well cared for.

Table 3.2 *Average infant mortality rates in areas of Lancashire 1901–10*

Textile areas	(per 1000)	Non-textile areas	(per 1000)
Bolton	148	West Derby	145
Bury	141	Prescot	
Rochdale	133	(Including St Helens)	144
Burnley	167	Wigan	166
Blackburn	148	Warrington	140
Preston	158	Barrow	119
		Lancaster	125
Average	149	Average	138

Sources: Register General reports 1901–10, cd. 8002 viii.

It has long been argued that the children of full-time working mothers suffered a much higher rate of infant mortality than did those of mothers staying at home [69; 36]. Recent work has suggested that statistically towns with a large percentage of married women in full-time work did not have *significantly* higher rates of infant mortality than did towns where few women were so employed [25; 76; 77]. The more interesting question is why there were such variations within the same category of towns.

Nineteenth-century criticisms of working women's abilities as housekeepers abound, but whatever the truth may have been then, there appears little evidence for believing that similar criticisms apply to the early twentieth century. There are indeed endless accounts of women working all day in the mill and then struggling through a large part of the night to keep their houses and families clean. Where working women did find difficulties was in feeding their families adequately. There was little time for preparing food and so working women often relied on convenience foods: either items which were quick to cook like chops and bacon, or food which was already cooked, fish and chips, bought bread, tripe, pies and cold meats. The drawback of this 'textile' diet was that it lacked variety, possibly lacked vitamins, and was comparatively quite expensive [76].

How successful were full-time working married women in improving their families' financial standing? As has been seen, this was the chief motivation in going out to work. In many families a woman working could at least double the family income. This is clear from the oral evidence, but the same evidence also indicates that full-time working wives were not so successful in improving the financial standing of their families as they or we might imagine, at any dates in this period. Ellen Barlee describes a visit to Lancashire in 1862:

> I learned that high as were the wages which the operatives earn, they are considerably reduced by the outlay which is necessary in consequence of the absence of the wife and mother from their domestic duties which must be deputed to others or performed at night. The former plan is generally adopted and a very large class of women derive their maintenance entirely by providing for the wants of mill hands and often earn more than the operatives themselves. [36, *63*]

Women in the oral history survey certainly worked at night, but they also paid for many services; some had washerwomen to do the washing, many had highly paid child-minders, and many had to pay the high cost of convenience foods. The net addition of a wife's earnings to the family income was thus much smaller than her actual wages. Yet it cannot be disputed that these wages, however reduced, helped to feed, clothe and house her family.

Unfortunately large numbers of married women in full-time work had an effect on wage rates of which the women themselves were unaware. There is evidence that the presence of a large number of married women depressed rates of men's wages, not just in the industries in which women were employed, but also in other spheres of employment in the surrounding geographical areas. The Board of Trade report for 1908 indicates that average labouring wages in the building and engineering trades in the textile towns in Lancashire were lower than in the non-textile towns [9]. In the inter-war years the Pilgrim Trust reported that men's wages had always been fixed at a lower level in the textile towns (and not merely in the textile industry) because it was assumed by employers that wives would work and earn wages [73]. Women in these areas were trapped in a vicious circle; they worked because they had to, but by working they ensured that they and other women would have to continue working [48].

The economic significance of married women's work in industries such as those manufacturing cotton, jute products, china and porcelain and the Midland metal industries is incalculable. They provided an essential element in the workforce and contributed to the prosperity long enjoyed by these industries. The effect the women had on the wider economy of the areas in which they worked is also important. On the positive side they improved the lot of child-minders, washerwomen, corner shops and manufacturers of convenience foods; negatively they probably lowered men's wages in various industries.

The vast majority of married women did not of course work fulltime. In 1911, in England and Wales, only 13.7 per cent of married and widowed women overall were in full-time paid employment. It would, of course, be absurd to say that the rest were economically inactive or unimportant. It is likely that the paid work done by these millions of women has failed to be enumerated in the census returns (see Chapter 1). And yet the work done by these women was useful, productive and important, both to the economies of their own families and for their communities in general. It has been calculated from oral evidence for the northwest of England in the period 1890–1940 that about 40 per cent of working-class women earned money on a part-time basis at some point in their married life [76]. Much more detailed research is needed to estimate how widespread this custom was both in time and in different areas. There are, however, some indications that this practice was widespread [7]. Part-time married women workers appear in Rowntree's survey of York [82], but are oddly absent from Pember Reeves' and Spring Rice's surveys [72; 87]. The range of work done by married women on a part-time basis was quite wide, and mirrored much of what was available on a fulltime basis. Thus they could take on casual dressmaking or alterations: a hem turned up, trousers let out and so on; while others produced food, such as pies, cooked hams and cakes, which they sold from their kitchen doors; others collected and sold firewood; and others again brewed herb beer. These 'retailers' sometimes expanded their business into full-scale 'parlour' shops and became proper and full-time shopkeepers; others restricted their efforts to selling on a small scale or for a limited period when there was a particular financial need. Personal services have been referred to previously such as child-minding, doing laundry and taking in lodgers, and some women went out to others' homes to clean, wash and occasionally to decorate. Others provided financial services of varying kinds: money was rarely loaned, for there was little extra available to enable women to do this, but various very small-scale local schemes to help others save and to make a small profit have been discovered. A woman, for example, might collect 6d a week from her neighbours, each week there would be a 'draw' in which the lucky person would receive the takings, less a certain commission for the organiser. No one could win more than once until everyone had 'won'. Others ran 'clubs' for holidays or Christmas. In the inter-war years many a working-class woman became an agent for mail order catalogues which gave her customers an opportunity of getting credit and herself some commission. In areas where pawnbrokers flourished, many women were ashamed of being seen visiting their premises and a local woman, again for a small fee, would undertake to visit the pawnbroker on behalf of several neighbours.

Most of these part-time workers worked from their own homes, and, unlike the out-workers described in Chapter 2, they can be described as self-employed. They tended to work at hours convenient to themselves and found it easier to fit in their housework than did full-time workers. Yet the part-time workers employed by others must not be overlooked, women such as the cleaners, cooks and washerwomen and also those who worked seasonally on the land; for example, the London hop-pickers, the Evesham fruit-pickers, the pea-pickers in Essex, Worcestershire, Leicestershire and Somerset [83]. Sometimes these women came from the town, for example the hop-pickers, and sometimes they were the wives of local labourers.

The economic value of this part-time work cannot be evaluated in monetary terms, but because so very many women were involved, it must have been of considerable significance to the economy at large. There is clear oral evidence that it was of the greatest value in many families, either in pushing the family's income above the poverty line or in tiding the family over a particularly difficult financial period.

All working-class married women, whether they worked full-time or part-time, or did not earn at all, nevertheless carried out a vast amount of work, again unquantifiable, but which was of the greatest economic and social value. They were cooks, dressmakers, house-cleaners, nursemaids, mothers and the controllers and balancers of family budgets [76]. If their services had been paid for, then either working-class families would have rapidly been reduced to destitution or employers would have found themselves with vastly increased wage bills for their male workers, and possible consequential financial ruin.

The important role of working-class women as consumers is examined by McKendrick [63]. He argues that during the early stages of the Industrial Revolution the purchases of working-class women stimulated demand for such consumer goods as textiles, clothing, pins, buckles and buttons, and pottery. Working-class women as consumers continued to play an important role throughout the nineteenth and twentieth centuries.

The majority of working-class wives aimed to balance the family budget and not get into debt. They worked heroically towards this end and it was due to their efforts that not only their own families, but also local shopkeepers and businesses, avoided financial disaster. Working-class wives did the family shopping and had a thorough knowledge of local prices. By their diligent pursuit of a bargain they were an active force in keeping prices competitive.

In some ways, though, women's attitudes actively reduced the growth of retail demand. Women were diligent in recycling goods instead of always buying new; orange boxes became furniture, and old clothes were converted into children's clothes, peg rugs or patchwork quilts. No food was wasted, stale bread was made into bread puddings, bones were made into broth and food scraps were given to or bartered with owners of hens and pigs.

Working-class women affected the pattern of retailing in other ways too. The period up to 1940 was the golden age of small local shops, which were patronised by working-class women because of their accessibility. Most of the shops gave credit and although the obtaining of it was generally regarded as a less desirable way of balancing a budget, it was essential for some families at some time, and for a minority of families at all times. Local shops also had a great social value, as places where the women of the neighbourhood met and exchanged news and gossip.

Small local shops also had disadvantages. They did not enjoy the benefits of wholesale bulk buying and many discerning shoppers came to believe that local prices were high and that the food was not as fresh as it might be. The popular alternatives were the Co-operative shops which were generally perceived as having goods of quality and with competitive prices. They also had the advantage of being very accessible since most working-class areas possessed one. For many their most important asset was the 'dividend', which provided a useful and painless way of saving money for expensive items like children's shoes. In general Co-operatives did *not* offer credit, although oral evidence suggests that some managers provided this service 'unofficially'. As each area's Co-operative stores were run according to the local Co-operative Society rules, it is difficult to generalise very much about them.

There are many difficulties and ambivalences in the whole area of working-class women and their use of credit [28]. As has already been indicated, the working-class ideal was to avoid credit and scrimp and scrape instead. This attitude must have inhibited the growth of widespread, widely used credit systems and it puts in doubt the existence of a 'consumer society' at least before 1914, in the sense of a society geared to the purchase of pianos, fur coats or cuddly toys. But it can be argued that during the First World War, although food was scarce, high earnings in some areas produced something akin to a consumer society.

Credit was, however, needed by some women at some time, and here inconsistencies of attitude are discernible. Women who would never have considered asking for credit from the grocer, green-grocer or butcher, had far fewer reservations about obtaining it for household linen or clothing. These credit schemes were often operated through the large number of 'Scotchmen', or door-to-door credit salesmen. One way these schemes operated was for the woman to be given a voucher worth £1 for which she paid £1 1s at the rate of 1s (5p) per week, and the voucher could be used to purchase goods at certain specified dealers. This system of gaining credit, to which was added mail order catalogue shopping in the inter-war period, became so widespread in certain areas that it was commented upon in official reports [10]. It would seem that retailing in clothing, linen and household goods was stimulated by this growth in the availability of credit. The effects of the granting of credit by small local shops on the volume of their trade and their profitability is more open to question, for its availability both attracted and repelled customers. Credit was necessary but some customers complained of being cheated, or of being debited with goods they never received. Disgruntled customers then went looking for 'fairer' shops. The shopkeepers themselves, in granting credit, walked a very fine line between, on the one hand, staying in business and making a living, and on the other, financial disaster. Unlike the 'Scotchmen' and the mail order catalogue organisers, local shops appear to have had a very unsystematic way of giving credit which simultaneously led to customer hostility and suspicion, and left them prone to bankruptcy. Oral evidence has revealed shopkeepers who had no idea how much was owing to them at any one time. It is impossible to assess the amount of credit given or the extent of the debt default in this period. It is probably unlikely that any estimate can be made since very few records survive from these small local shops. It is clear, however, that in times of particular hardship, as for example, at the time of the slump in the early 1920s in Barrow, many small shops were bankrupted; housewives could no longer pay off their debts and the shopkeepers in turn defaulted on theirs.

Pawnbroking was part of the credit system. In North Lancashire visits to the pawnbrokers were a last resort, usually made by the very poor. But pawnbrokers played an important part in some women's budgeting and were of greater significance in some areas than others [91].

Working-class women also had an important, but as yet unexplored and unquantified, effect as consumers on the housing market. Women, because of their control of the family budget and because the house was where they spent the greatest part of their lives, had a particular interest both in getting the best value for money in their housing, and also for improving their conditions wherever and whenever possible. Oral evidence indicates that in Barrow at the beginning of the century, women, often with husbands in very poorly paid jobs, were instrumental in buying their family a home, calculating that repaying a loan was cheaper than paying rent. This trend of women pushing their families into being owner occupiers continued throughout the period. In the inter-war period there is clear evidence of women choosing to spend their surplus income (and for those in work real incomes began to rise in this period) on better housing [76; 59, 3]. Some bought homes, while others sought out better rented properties with amenities like baths and a hot water system and chose to pay a higher rent; others again spent more on furnishings, fittings and decorating. Much more research needs to be done on the effect of women's decision-making, both on the housing market and on related commercial enterprises such as the manufacture of furniture, carpeting and furnishing fabrics.

The work of working-class married women has been ignored by many social and economic historians; but this very brief outline is intended to suggest that, whether full or part-time, paid or unpaid, at home or in the community, this work was in itself of great social and economic importance and in turn affected many areas of economic activity.

4

Protection and restriction: government, employers and unions

This chapter is concerned with women's working conditions, wages and their status as workers. It attempts to outline some of the improvements made in women's working conditions during the period and the parts played in those changes by government, employers and workers. The period is long and complex; therefore no attempt has been made to move chronologically through the century. Instead certain themes are examined with a particular concentration on the First World War when so many of the issues raised by women's work came into sharp focus.

Both contemporaries and more recent historians have found much to criticise about women's working conditions but their emphasis has varied over time. Observers at the beginning of the period, for example, were particularly worried about the hours women worked and their physical environment. Modern feminist historians have tended to concentrate on the low status of women workers and their poor pay in comparison with that of men. What have often been missing from these debates are the views and attitudes of the working-class women themselves. The legislators who passed laws governing many aspects of women's work were predominantly middle and upper class and always male (until after the First World War). Writers and historians have rarely been manual workers themselves and even the best-known women of the last quarter of the nineteenth century, who worked to establish women's unions, were middle class.

If women's working conditions and status were to be improved, there would appear to have been three main agencies who could have independently and/or co-operatively achieved this improvement: the government, the employers, and the workers. There were employers who independently and for philanthropic reasons improved the conditions of their workers, both men and women. The Quaker firms of Cadbury and Rowntree are examples of this. They were, however, in a small minority: most employers acted for improvement only when forced to do so by one or both of the other agencies. For reasons of space it is outside the scope of this chapter to develop the theme of philanthropic employers, and the main emphasis will therefore be on the more reluctant kind.

As seen in Chapter 1, there was much disquiet voiced in Parliament at the beginning of the period about the role of women in certain industries. Some critics were influenced by notions of philanthropy and others were deeply affected by the domestic idyll. These attitudes persisted and Parliament passed a mass of legislation which attempted to regulate and improve women's working conditions. The Mines Act of 1842 forbade women to work underground but, apart from this single prohibition, legislation did not affect the actual locations where women were permitted to work. Women continued to be employed above ground in the mining industry, in dirty and often dangerous conditions. It was 1972 before the last two pitbrow lasses in England (at Whitehaven) were declared redundant [50, *230*]. In 1911 in England there were 2843 women coal workers and in Scotland 2396, which represents virtually no decline from the estimated total of 6500 women working in the mines in 1840 [50, *250*].

The Factory Act of 1844 classified women as 'protected persons'. Those in trades covered by the Act (that is textiles), had their working day reduced to 12 hours and were excluded from night work. The 10 Hour Act of 1847 reduced women's working day still further to ten hours (although this was increased again to $10\frac{1}{2}$ in 1850). A long series of Factory Acts in 1853, 1860, 1864, 1867, 1878, 1891 and 1895 extended the protection given to women in textiles to other industries; for example, those making pottery, china, glass and paper, and those dealing with tobacco and gutta-percha. The 1867 Act attempted to define a factory by saying its requirements applied to any establishment employing 50 or more workers. The 1891 and 1895 Acts, in particular, attempted to control working conditions in small workshops and sweat shops which were two of the more difficult areas to supervise. In 1896 legislation became effective which limited women to 30 days overtime a year, with a maximum of three days in any one week. The 1906 and 1913 Shop Acts laid down maximum hours for shop-workers and the 1906 Act brought to an end the living-in system (see Chapter 2). Laundry workers whose places of work were hot, steamy and dirty and who worked very long hours, were included in the regulations in 1907. The suffering match girls were finally and positively helped in 1908 when an Act forbade the use of white phosphorus in the manufacture of matches. Phosphorus had caused some of the girls to develop a horrible disease known as 'phossy' jaw. There remained the difficult and almost intractable problem of women working either in very small workshops or in their own homes as out-workers and home-workers. In 1909 the Trade Boards Act established wages boards on which both employers and employees were to be represented. These Boards were to settle the rates of earnings and hours of work in four trades: lacemaking, chainmaking, paper box making, and wholesale and bespoke tailoring. In 1913 six more trades were brought under statutory wage control and many more were added in 1918.

Yet the home remained a place about which lawmakers hesitated to legislate and in which it was very difficult to enforce legislation even when passed. The great majority of women worked in their own or other people's homes and it is clear that throughout the period under review legislation, while helping out-workers, could not solve all their difficulties and, for housewives and domestic servants, did not make any attempt at regulation.

It is impossible to infer or describe a coherent working-class attitude to women's working conditions and particularly to women's status as paid workers. There were many contradictory positions, not just between men and women, but between man and man and woman and woman. (Some of these attitudes and assumptions have been outlined in Chapter 1.) Men had long held contradictory views. Some supported the idea of women working, usually because they could see the value of this work to themselves: for example, Scottish miners, before the Mines Act, preferred to have their wives working with them in a family team, rather than having to subcontract tasks to strangers [56]. Men in the textile areas often welcomed the addition to the family budget that came from their wives' earnings. But men also saw working women as a threat to their own work and status. Many believed that only a limited amount of work was available and they suspected that allowing women to share what work there was would cause some families to be without pay as a result of others taking more than their share. The only solutions appeared to be to forbid women to work at all for wages, or to confine them to jobs with low status and low wages. In 1842 the Yorkshire Short Time Committee, in a particularly blatant display of an attitude shared by many, demanded not merely that women should work only 'short' time but also that all married women should be banned from paid work while their husbands were employed. Some trades and crafts attempted to ban women from membership and hence from work; the London tailors did this in the 1830s, but by the 1840s they were using women as unskilled labour for some tailoring tasks, and thus keeping down their costs. Yet they also complained that sweated female labour undercut their wages. They thus faced the classic dilemma of all male workers. If women were forced, by men, to take the lowest paid positions, there was the constant danger of their undercutting men's wages. But if women's wages were raised was that not tantamount to admitting that they did an equal job alongside the men? This dilemma was not, of course, solved within the period 1840–1940 although it had been clearly visible as early as 1840.

Women's attitudes to their status and conditions of work varied very much: distinct attitudes and groups were readily discernible both at the beginning and throughout the period (see Chapter 1). These attitudes are represented and symbolised in women's relationships (or lack of them) with trades unions and other groups whose aim was the improvement of workers' lives. Some historians, for example Sheila Lewenhak [56], have asked why so few women were actively involved in trade unions. Deborah Thom prefers to enquire why so many joined against considerable odds [94].

Obviously what women did and did not do was affected by the attitudes of men. Some women were hostile to the whole area of women working for wages and a minority of these were vocal in their hostility. During the Preston spinners' strike of 1853 women took part, although the mule spinners were exclusively men, in support of a demand that employers pay wages sufficiently high to enable operatives to keep their wives at home in comfort, without the necessity of sending them to work in the mill [56, *61*]. This was an example of men and women uniting in their demands for men to be paid a family wage. Obviously women who believed so fervently that a woman's place was in the home would not join any form of trade union; although they would and did support male unionists.

There were many working women who did not belong to a union because there was no union for them to belong to. This was particularly true of the many thousands of women in domestic service who remained non-unionised throughout the period. There were also other women who, although working in an industry where there was a union, felt unable to join, either because the union seemed to be male-dominated or because, as married women, they had little time or energy for union affairs. Certainly inbuilt into British trade unions and clearly visible after their revival following the repeal of the Combination Acts in 1824 and 1825, was an acceptance of a hierarchical system intended to protect those holding the 'best' jobs. Union members were determined to safeguard status, work and prices for both goods and wages. As women rarely held the 'best' jobs and were frequently to be found amongst the worst paid, they were unlikely to do well in most unions [56]. The hostility of craftsmen towards women was not obviously different from their hostility to unskilled men when they felt threatened by competitors.

The belief that somehow unions were concerned solely with improving men's conditions and wages not only prevented women from joining some unions (and statistically throughout the period it is clear that women played a less active role in trade unions than did men), it also ensured that many women who did belong took only a very apathetic part. They paid their dues and expected the union's help if they had an individual dispute with management, but that appeared to be the total extent of their involvement [60, 96–7]. An enquiry carried out by the Women's Trade Union & Provident League (WTUL) in 1900 into the problems of organising women in unions showed that there was little difficulty in finding women willing to join unions in a period when more unions were opening the membership to women. What was a difficulty was the turnover in women's membership and their apparent lack of staying power [24]. This question is examined in depth by Joanna Bornat with particular reference to women in the General Union of Textile Workers [14].

There was, however, another group of women, who far from being apathetic union members, were active and worked with men, if not quite as equals at least with some degree of co-operation. Male and female weavers, acting together, in 1853, in the Blackburn Association of Cotton Weavers, negotiated the first district price list for weaving, which endured for some years. This was a notable achievement [56]. In general weavers continued to act co-operatively, but women rarely rose to positions of responsibility [24].

There were, also, instances of unionised women going on strike alongside their male colleagues. In Yorkshire, for example, the Manningham Mill strike of 1890 against wage reductions involved many women plush weavers. Although the strike failed it provided a great stimulus to the growth of the Independent Labour Party [14, *215*]. There are other examples of women being involved in strikes in the pre-First World War period [56].

It is indeed possible that, as Jane Lewis argues, women's passivity has been greatly exaggerated [58, *183*]. Striking was not the only form of labour protest open to them; indeed going on strike was a comparatively rare form. Oral evidence from working-class women records arguments with overlookers and managers as ways of employees 'getting their own back' and other forms of protest, notably leaving and finding another job [76, *46–9*]. Women clerical workers appear to have adopted similar tactics [98].

In the nineteenth century there were some women who believed passionately that women needed to join women-only organisations to work for the improvement of the lot of their sex. In the middle of the century, when it has been suggested that women were particularly inactive in union affairs, they can be found in female friendly societies which provided mutual help and insurance schemes for women in many trades: there were female Foresters, female Oddfellows, female Rechabites, and so on. It could be argued that these were simply branches of men's societies and in any case did little for actual working conditions, but their existence demonstrated women's ability to organise for a stated purpose.

The last quarter of the nineteenth century saw a much more active female involvement in trade unionism and what are most usually described are the all-female unions. Their pioneer was a remarkable woman, Emma Paterson (1848–86), and she and her successors showed an outstanding flair for publicity and public relations and notable qualities of leadership. They were not, however, of working-class origin and it has been suggested that they did not always represent what working-class women themselves wanted. Emma Paterson was a bookbinder by trade but the London Consolidated Bookbinders Society refused to admit women members, including Emma Paterson herself. After her marriage she and her husband went to the United States where she found women-only unions. She was determined to campaign for the same in the United Kingdom as she was convinced that there was no prospect of men allowing women into their unions as equals. She therefore aimed to promote the establishment of all-women unions under the umbrella of her Women's Protection and Provident League (WPPL). She sought and obtained support from middle-class women who shared her views and who tended to dominate the women's trade union movement for many years thereafter.

Emma Paterson had a rather controversial attitude to government legislation about working conditions. She opposed it, arguing that classifying women with children was degrading and implied that women were helpless and unable to help themselves. She was convinced that only by combining in trade unions would women improve their wages and conditions of work. The WPPL was successful in promoting the establishment of all-female unions among bookbinders, upholsterers and shirt and collar makers, dressmakers and milliners; in 1886 it was calculated that the total membership was 2500, about half of whom lived in London. The League advocated the avoidance of industrial disputes and made no provision out of its funds for strike pay. By the time of Emma Paterson's death in 1886 the League claimed to have established between 30 and 40 women's societies. One of their biggest successes in her lifetime was in persuading the TUC to accept women delegates to their conference in 1875 [86] and by 1881 there were ten such representatives. Emma Paterson also campaigned, successfully, for the appointment of female factory inspectors (the first being appointed in 1893). She saw inspectors as an alternative to protective legislation for female workers.

After the death of Emma Paterson, leadership of the WPPL for the rest of the century passed to Lady Emilia Dilke. She was generous in her financial donations and very able in publicising the cause of women workers. Unlike Emma Paterson she supported government legislation for the improvement of working conditions and with considerable energy spread the work of the WPPL over a much wider area than had previously been possible, for most of the early women's unions were London-based. The WPPL changed its name to the Women's Trade Union & Provident League in 1889. The new name was symbolic of Lady Dilke's interest in working with existing male and mixed trade unions as well as through women-only societies.

Lady Dilke was succeeded as leader of the WTUL in 1903 by Mary MacArthur, a Scotswoman of genius. Like her predecessor, Mary MacArthur had tried to enrol women as members in male trade unions, as well as into unions of their own. But in view of the refusal of certain male unions to admit women, the WTUL (not itself a union) called in 1906 for a General Labour Union for women, open to all women either belonging to an unorganised trade or not admitted to other appropriate unions. This new union was called the National Federation of Women Workers (NFWW) and in its first year had seventeen branches with a total 2250 members. By 1914 it had 20,000 members and had become affiliated to the TUC.

It is difficult to estimate the success of the WPPL and later the WTUL. Their direct influences in the establishment of all-women unions can be noted but they also had undoubted influence, firstly in increasing women's awareness of the importance of trade union activity, secondly in stimulating government legislation in the pre-First World War period, and thirdly on the declared policies of the TUC, which increasingly supported equal pay resolutions.

We cannot be precise about why so many women were willing to join trade unions in the decade before the First World War. Deborah Thom argues that the social, political and economic climate in which the women lived – for example the campaign against sweating, the introduction of social welfare reform by the Liberal government, the women's suffrage movement, and the fall in real wages – encouraged women's participation in trade unions at that time. 'This increase [i.e. in membership] arose from a multiplicity of factors against which the individual contribution of leaders needs to be measured' [94, *262*]. The WTUL's activities must have been influential even though most of those women who became members of a union in fact joined mixed unions. In 1886 it was estimated that 36,980 women were members of trade unions: this rose to 142,000 in 1892 and 433,000 in 1913, a dramatic increase of 300 per cent between 1892 and 1913.

Significant as these figures are they must be put in perspective. The 1911 census reported 4,830,734 women as occupied in paid employment in England and Wales. Thus less than 10 per cent of women were members of a union as compared with nearly 30 per cent of male workers. About half of the women unionists were textile workers, who were all in mixed unions, and it cannot be merely coincidence that the textile unions were relatively successful in unionising women. The textile industry was an industry where women winders, carders and weavers had long been regarded by male workers as having some degree of equality; and women had been accepted as leaders in the textile unions as early as the 1860s.

Women's working conditions and status changed radically, although temporarily, during the First World War. This period provides an opportunity to look again at the prevailing problems of women workers and the many conflicting attitudes held by men and women, government, employers and unions towards female employment [17; 93; 94].

During the First World War there was a tremendous need for extra labour for such tasks as making munitions, running the transport system, working on the land or helping in the engineering trades. As millions of men, initially volunteers and later as conscripts, joined the army, it was obvious that women would be compelled to take their places. Their labour was needed, but set against this overwhelming need was the strongly held attitude that a woman's place was in the home caring for the family [17]. The clash between national need and this deeply entrenched belief was not resolved on a long-term basis.

Once the war was under way there was a great increase in work for women in industries which had already traditionally employed them; notable in textiles, for uniforms, and the manufacture of footwear. By 1915 they were also to be found in jobs traditionally done by men, for example, as clerks, or tram conductors and drivers. By the middle of 1915 the issue which was to prove the most contentious came to the fore: the question of substitution or 'dilution' whereby large numbers of women took jobs in industry which had previously been done by men. By 1917 the *Labour Gazette* estimated that one in three working women was directly replacing a male industrial worker. In some specific industries the increase in the number of women workers was dramatic: Woolwich Arsenal, which produced munitions, employed 125 women in 1914, but by 1917 these had increased to 28,000 [93].

Almost everything that can be written about women's work during the First World War is, or was, controversial. It is not even clear, for example, how many women were involved in war work, or indeed how many women worked at all. Braybon suggests that in July 1914 3,276,000 women were in full-time paid work [17]. By April 1918, this figure had risen to an estimated 4,808,500. These figures present difficulties, since the census for England and Wales gives the total number of females occupied in 1911 as 4,839,734 [Census 1911 Occupations 15B]. If Braybon's figures are accepted, then fewer women were working in 1918 than in 1911: this would seem unlikely and must mean that the estimates of women in work for both 1914 and 1918 are much too low. But however much the estimate is realistically increased, it is obvious that the majority of women even by this time were not in paid, full-time work. The 1911 census gave 10,026,379 females as unoccupied or retired (a figure which included children). Despite the newspaper stories, and indeed propaganda, of the time, there was not a vast army of women working in factories or on the land. Oral evidence reminds us that in fact only a small proportion of women worked in munitions. It is clear that others tried it, and found it difficult and dangerous, hated the work and abandoned it very quickly. Others, notably married women, did not even begin, believing that their place was still at home. Some became desperate because of the smallness of the army allowance, but they seemed to prefer traditional kinds of work at home, such as taking in lodgers or sewing, to going to the munitions factory. On the other hand, oral evidence also reveals that the women who went into munitions, and stayed with them, very often enjoyed the work and the camaraderie of the other women, and appreciated escaping from domestic service. Other women enjoyed the opportunity to move out of factories into office work.

It is clear from Braybon's work that the women who were in full-time work were ambivalent in their attitudes towards it. Some wanted equal pay for equal work with men. Others wanted lower rates of pay, either because they appeared to believe that they did a less good job than the men, or because they believed that earning equal pay would automatically mean losing their jobs when in competition with men at the conclusion of hostilities.

Employers also had contradictory aims and policies. They wished to complete orders as efficiently and as speedily as possible, with the lowest possible costs and the highest possible profits. But whatever was done by the employers had to meet with union approval, for their power and influence had grown appreciably in the early part of the twentieth century [71; 17; 56]. Employers' actions also had to accord with government legislation.

Employers usually tried to avoid replacing a skilled man directly with a woman worker. This pleased the unions, who generally shared with the employers the idea that women could not do the same work as a skilled man. If possible, employers also avoided a direct substitution in order to reduce costs. If it could be 'proved' that women were not being directly substituted for men, then they would be paid lower wages and there would be little room for argument. Various methods of substitution were devised, an unskilled man might be promoted to the skilled man's place; a small number of women might be used; sometimes a large group of women were substituted for a smaller group of men; or skilled tasks were broken down into a series of unskilled ones. Barbara Drake described how a complex job of engineering, previously done by one man, was divided into 22 separate operations to be performed by no less than 22 women [17].

These various forms of substitution were generally accepted by the male-dominated trade unions. Outside this general agreement, however, there were still the same ambiguous and contradictory attitudes towards women workers. Some unions took in women for the first time; for example, the National Union of Railwaymen in 1915, and the Electrical Trade Union in 1916. Mixed unions, like the Amalgamated Society of Carpenters and Joiners, continued to admit women as before. Others continued to refuse women membership. The Preston Operatives and Spinners Association continued to rebuff women who applied to work the mules or join the union.

Skilled men were ambivalent about substitution. They were opposed to one woman replacing one skilled man, since the implications of such an action were obviously unthinkable! They were, however, unhappy about the breaking down of skilled work into a series of unskilled processes, fearing an ultimate loss of job and devaluation in terms both of status and of wages of their practical skill. This was not an unjustified fear. There were new engineering works in the Midlands, making motor cycles, for example, where women who had not served an engineering apprenticeship were employed. They were regarded as 'unskilled' and paid as such. There were not many job opportunities for skilled men in these factories. Skilled men faced the old but still critical dilemma of not being able either to accept women as their peers or to tolerate them as unskilled workers: both ways women workers were seen as a threat. Some men, of perhaps more extreme opinions, continued with the attitude noted in the mid-nineteenth century that the only way out of this dilemma was to exclude women from paid work altogether. John Wadsworth, for example, the General Secretary of the Yorkshire Miners Association, wrote to the *Yorkshire Evening Post* in June 1916 about the proposal to allow women to work on the Yorkshire pit banks as they already did in other areas, arguing:

We think that a woman's place is at home, looking after the home, husband and family and if she is a young woman she ought to be learning something better than pit bank work. [17, *74*]

In general neither employers, trade unions, nor indeed some women, could believe that women were capable of doing a job of equal worth to that of a man. It is difficult to know just how well women workers performed during the First World War. The conclusions of the report compiled by A. W. Kirkcaldy in 1917 were that whether women were as good as men at skilled work depended entirely on the selection and training of the women and their subsequent management. He concluded that women's only inherent disadvantage was their inferior physical strength [17].

At the end of the war, and with the demobilisation of the troops, it became clear that neither the government, the unions nor the employers were willing or able to protect women's jobs, and/or increase their opportunities. The widespread and sometimes hysterical gratitude, as expressed in the popular newspapers, for women's war work was quickly forgotten. Even the women workers themselves seem to have largely believed that it was 'right' to return either to their pre-war jobs or to their homes.

The only women who retained the 'gains' made during the First World War were those in clerical jobs. One old man remarked of Lancaster's largest firm that: 'there were no females in the offices until the First World War' [79, Transcript Mr P.I.L.]. It is clear that not only in those offices but in countless others the women stayed on and continued to fill more and more clerical jobs. It is unlikely that the war was the sole cause for this extension of job opportunities for women. Clerical work had been changing for some years before the First World War, and from being seen as work suitable for men, it had increasingly been regarded as work fit only for women.

Other women who had been employed during the war found themselves in an unenviable position. About half of those who had made up the increase in women workers voluntarily withdrew from the labour market, either because they genuinely preferred to be at home or because they regarded it as their patriotic duty to make way for the men returning from the war [17]. Other women were dismissed, especially from the munitions works which had no more markets for their goods. What was to become of these unemployed women? It is clear, from both words and actions, that Government and unions wanted them back in the home or confined to traditional women's jobs. Braybon considers that women's positions in industry actually worsened after the war. They were often regarded with open hostility by men who had realised for the first time that women were fully capable of carrying out jobs previously perceived as men's, thus presenting a real challenge. The trade union newspaper, *The Democrat* made it clear throughout 1919 that although trade unionists paid lip service to the rights of women to education and equal pay, there was no determination, or indeed wish, to change the *status quo* which continued to see women as dependent on a male breadwinner. Joanna Bornat wrote of the women in the Yorkshire woollen industry; 'Wartime production demanded the temporary promotion of women to indispensability. Peacetime saw a return to marginality, dependency and domesticity' [14, *228*]. Her words could describe the experience of nearly all women workers at that time.

The government was willing to set up training schemes for unemployed women but only for traditional 'women's' trades like domestic service. Little sympathy and much hostility was otherwise shown to the unemployed women. Attacks, for example, were made on the granting of unemployment benefit. In 1920 only 40 per cent of unemployed women received benefit [17], but even those lucky enough to receive benefit had it cut to 15s (75p) a week and this was refused unless the unemployed woman agreed to make herself available for domestic work; once there she was not insured, and therefore not eligible for future unemployment pay.

Historians have sometimes waxed lyrical about the differences made in women's lives by the First World War, but for working-class women most of these changes disappeared after 1918, and in employment their position could hardly be said to have improved or changed dramatically since before the war. The census of 1921 showed that the proportion of gainfully employed females (over 10 years old) was 30.8 per cent as compared with 32.3 per cent in 1911.

5
Conclusion

The inter-war period, which is still rather under-researched by historians, can in some ways be seen as a summary of much of what had happened (or not happened) in the sphere of women's work since 1840.

On the positive side, the range of wage-earning jobs open to working-class women widened. In 1840 women had worked in mills, potteries, factories, workshops and houses. The growth in shop-work and clerical work observable before the First World War continued in the inter-war period (see Chapter 2) and there were also new opportunities in certain branches of engineering, notably in the newer electrical and smaller engineering factories. It was widely assumed by employers that women workers did not mind repetitive jobs or machine-minding and were very good at small intricate tasks. By the end of 1938 there were 60,000 women in engineering, 26,000 in the manufacture of cycles and aircraft, 76,000 in the making of electric cables, and 75,000 in the metal industries [86; 58, *182*]. These 'new' jobs which women did were simply not regarded as men's work. (Ironically these attitudes to women's work finally took on a different meaning in the 1980s when this kind of work continued to recruit women while men skilled in the old 'heavy' industries such as mining, iron and steel found themselves unemployed.)

In the period between 1840 and the First World War there had been many improvements in women's working conditions: working hours had been reduced, minimum wages fixed in the sweated trades, and there had been legislation to regulate some of the worst physical environments in which women worked (for example in the match factories and in laundries). In the inter-war

Table 5.1 *Average wages of men and women in shillings per week, 1924–35*

Industry	1924		1933		1935	
	Men	Women	Men	Women	Men	Women
Engineering	51.1	26.3	50.4	26.8	55.0	28.0
Textiles	51.0	28.6	48.0	26.9	49.2	27.5
Clothing and footwear	54.8	26.9	53.6	26.9	54.3	27.8
Food, drink, tobacco	58.0	27.9	57.5	28.0	56.6	26.6

Sources: [16; 86].

period, these gains were not lost but new improvements in working conditions proved difficult to attain (although it could be argued that the new office workers had much more congenial working conditions than did, for example, cotton weavers). In 1919 the International Labour Organisation (ILO) condemned the two-shift system introduced during the war but the British government refused to legislate against it. In 1927 the TUC's Women's Committee called for a cut in the working day for women from 10 to 9 hours and for an end to the shift system but this was not achieved during the period. Above all, the women failed to achieve equal pay with men with equal work. The revolutionary statement introduced by Clementina Black, Secretary of the WTUL, to the TUC in 1886, remained a dead letter:

That in the opinion of Congress, it is desirable in the interests of both men and women that in trades where women do the same work as men, they shall receive the same payment. [56, *91*]

Some male trade unionists at the TUC in the inter-war period called upon unions to make all-out efforts to achieve equal pay for equal work but their call went unheeded, and women workers continued to be low-paid in comparison with men in the same industry. According to Bowley, women's wages were approximately 50 per cent of those of men (see Table 5.1). Some of the complexities of the equal pay debate were analysed by Jane Lewis [58, *200–5*].

Women who looked back from 1940 to 1840 would have been

Table 5.2 *Women's union membership 1918–39*

	1918	1933	1939
Distributive	62,000	58,800	54,119
Textiles	163,000	43,417	45,897
Clothing	88,500	48,202	78,604
Cotton	260,000	149,264	109,000
Food, drink, tobacco	7,000	2,371	5,284
Printing, bookbinding	54,000	29,296	39,191
Boot and shoe	28,000	24,917	34,095
General and municipal workers	216,000	—	43,321

Sources: [16; 86].

justified in seeing that they had contributed in many ways to the improvements in working conditions which had taken place. But they might also have reflected that women's position in the labour movement remained generally less important and less influential than that of men. There were, of course, as there had been in the nineteenth and early twentieth centuries, women who fought hard for improvements in the conditions and status of working women. There is evidence of women workers enthusiastically joining unions in the car industry and perhaps more remarkable was their record of involvement in strikes which was far in excess of their numerical involvement in the industry. In other words they were more likely than the men were to go on strike [96; 54]. Women's militancy went in fact beyond the motor industry [54].

However, if a more general and national picture is drawn, women played a minor role in trade union activities. As has been shown, the leaders of the WTUL before the war increasingly encouraged women to join mixed unions. After the war both men and women trade unions embarked on a period of amalgamation, presumably working on the assumption that through unification would come strength. The NFWW amalgamated with the National Union of General Workers in 1921 and in the same year the WTUL became part of the TUC as the Women Workers' group. But these moves did not solve the problems of women's position and status in trade unions. There was a marked decline in women's trade union membership between the wars (see Table 5.2); this was partly the result of industrial depression, although improving trade conditions did not produce markedly more women unionists in the 1930s. The decline was also due to the continuing difficulties of women in trade unions.

Women's problems in trade unions were the familiar ones which had been seen repeatedly earlier in this period [24]. They earned less than their male colleagues did and paid smaller union contributions. They consequently received lower rates of benefit and were regarded, and perhaps regarded themselves, as second-class union members. There were some exceptions: women in the Potteries were active as union dues collectors and often their influence within the family was very important as to whether a worker joined the union or not [97]. In general, however, women took a minor part in the management of most unions and the rank and file were generally apathetic. Oral evidence indicates that women textile workers, with few exceptions, saw union membership as an insurance against the time of a dispute between themselves and management. Women continued to regard unions as male-orientated and male-dominated institutions; and yet there was no move to reintroduce the all-female union. The women who were prominent in union affairs continued to believe that the improvement in the conditions and status of women workers lay through their membership of mixed trade unions [56; 86]. It should be stressed that for the largest group of women workers, that is, the domestic servants, trade unionism continued to have little personal relevance as they remained non-unionised. (An attempt was made to establish a union of domestic servants in 1937 but it was calculated that only 1500 out of a possible 1,500,000 joined.)

Attitudes to women's work in the inter-war years appear to have been little different to those found in earlier generations. It would seem that the *majority* of people, which included working-class men and women as well as employers and legislators, believed that a woman's place, and especially a married woman's place, was in the home, not in the factory, shop or office. Indeed for the working-class woman, the inter-war period saw a full flowering of the domestic ideology. It is tempting to ask whether this was because of, or in spite of their working experiences in the First World War.

Unmarried women could be expected to work for wages outside the home but this was regarded by women, and by others, as simply a useful way of filling in time until marriage. It was also a way of earning money and of contributing to their families' budgets. Even if a woman had wanted to continue work after marriage this was impossible to do in many jobs, because employers operated a marriage bar. The ban in teaching is well known, but less well known are the policies of *individual* employers who refused, for example, to employ married shop assistants and typists (these marriage bars are traceable through oral evidence but much more research needs to be done).

Some women did continue to work after marriage, notably in the textile and pottery industries. They appear to have worked because of financial necessity and their ambition was to stop work and to be at home; they saw their liberation as away from full-time work and towards domesticity.

Smaller families and more convenient houses should have given these women time and opportunity to get out of the home, but as the domestic ideology strengthened, so too the standards of house cleaning, home decoration and child care were raised [59, 4]. What time was left was spent in creative pursuits like embroidery and crochet, often of a very high standard. It is impossible, even with the help of oral evidence, to assess whether women really chose and enjoyed this kind of life or whether they accepted it because it was the 'norm'. Women express discontent with their lot during this period but they rarely complain of having wanted to be in full-time work and of somehow having been prevented from doing so. Another reason for women choosing to be at home was the rising standard of living of families where father was in full-time work; rising real wages meant that many women no longer felt the financial imperative to go out to work to supplement the family income. Needless to say for the millions of women whose husbands were unemployed or sick or absent for any reason, there was no choice but to find some wage-earning work [76].

Because the majority of women saw their place as in the home, not just in the inter-war period but throughout the century from 1840–1940, it is important to look at the work done by women in the home, because this remained the most typical work done by working-class women throughout the period. Feminist historians have rightly criticised the historical tendency to define woman's role in the labour market in terms of her familial role, a process which devalued her paid work. It would be a great pity if conversely woman's low status in the world of paid work led historians to devalue her valuable and important work as housewife and mother.

Bibliographical appendix

In the first chapter of this book I expressed some doubts about attempting to give an overview of women's work in this period and wrote, 'Generalisations are inevitable as are aggregated data. These tend to obscure very important differences between areas and indeed between towns.' Some of the books about women's work which have appeared since 1988 tend by and large to concentrate on particular areas and/or case studies. These are important in their own right, but also provide material for future 'overviews' of women's work. It is possible to see that they have certain common themes, women's waged work was generally low paid in comparison to that of men, and it was gendered. These recent works also continue to recognise and to explore the complex interrelationship between women's work in the home and family and their position in the labour market.

Carl Chinn's *They worked all their lives; women of the urban poor in England, 1880–1939* (Manchester University Press, 1988) is based on the lives of poor women in Birmingham, and illustrates clearly the interconnectedness between women as wives, mothers, family budget controllers and workers for wages both at home and in the outside world.

Women and industrialisation: gender at work in nineteenth-century England (Polity Press, 1990) by Judy Lown is a detailed and probably definitive history of the work and home lives of the men and women in the Courtaulds Silk Mill at Halstead, Essex in the nineteenth century. Whereas Carl Chinn explores the concept of matriarchy, Lown uses her historical material to analyse the concept of patriarchy and the ways in which it shaped the organisation of work and the relationship between employers and employees and male and female workers. She emphasises the low status and low wages of the latter (with the exception of the skilled women weavers). The work of Chinn and Lown might suggest a way forward in the debates about matriarchy and patriarchy. While it would be difficult to suggest that the labour market was *not* organised on patriarchal principles, when the family economy, and women's role in it, is examined, it becomes more possible to describe matriarchies.

Women's work and the family economy in historical perspective edited by Pat Hudson and W. R. Lee (Manchester University Press, 1990) is an ambitious attempt to look at women's work before, during and after the Industrial Revolution and in Europe as well as in Great Britain. It combines both an overview and case studies. The introduction by the two editors provides a masterly analysis which in turn establishes a framework into which the succeeding 'case studies' can be fitted. These clearly indicate the changing role of women in the family economy, not only over time but from area to area; the nature of local customs and the local economy being particularly important, as well as national laws. Chapters which have particular relevance to the subject of women's work 1840–1940 are 'Kinship, labour and enterprise: the Staffordshire pottery industry 1890–1920' by Richard Whipp; 'Women in a car town, Coventry 1920–45' by Linda Grant; 'Unemployment and the making of the feminine during the Lancashire cotton famine' by Clare Evans; and 'The hidden economy of docklands families: Liverpool in the 1930s' by Pat Ayres. On the whole the book concentrates on the interface of women's roles in the domestic and the formal 'official' economies and rather neglects the informal unstructured economies (described in Chapter 3 of this book) in which women played a crucial role and which in time affected the wellbeing of so many families. The chapter by Pat Ayres is therefore especially valuable.

Richard Whipp writes much more fully about the pottery industry in *Patterns of labour, work and social change in the pottery industry* (Routledge 1990). Despite women providing much of the labour force in this important industry they do not merit a chapter to themselves. The book's main thrust is about the complexities of the industry itself. The attempt to place it in its social setting within the local community is not as authoritative as the analysis of the industry. The evidence Whipp uses to illustrate the important role of concern in the home, family and community is in itself identical to that from towns and different industrial structures. This might suggest that explanations of working-class social life need to be sought in a wider sphere than simply in the local work place. A rather more insightful and comprehensive view of women's work and lives in the pottery industry is to be found in *Missuses and mould-runners* by Jacqueline Sarsby (Open University Press, 1988). This is based on oral interviews with women pottery workers and reflects on their work and lives in the interwar period (and up to the 1980s).

An important book which looks at more than one ending and which offers an overview is Miriam Glucksman's *Women assemble. Women workers and the new industries in inter-war Britain* (Routledge, 1990). In it she examines the question of why working-class women became the main labour force on assembly lines in the industries producing new consumer goods in the 1920s and 1930s. She discovered that particular kinds of women were recruited, young, single, industrially inexperienced with no formal skills. This group was much less able or likely to bargain over wages and conditions than older skilled unionised male workers. There was a sexual division of labour in these new rigid industries with women on the assembly lines and men working everywhere else. This new group of industrial workers did however earn more than if they had been domestic servants (as many would have been earlier in the period) and these earnings made a significant contribution to the family economy. The family budget was becoming more able to afford finished manufactured goods rather than the raw materials upon which the women of the family had previously to work (unpaid) to make them usable. (For example making cotton into clothes and flour into bread and cakes.)

Another book which looks rather differently at women's work in the inter-war period is Deirdre Beddoe's '*Back to home and duty*', *women between the wars 1918–1939* (Pandora, 1989). Here the all-pervasive model of domestic ideology is presented as being the only one women were expected to follow. Given the number of single women who worked (as evidenced in Glucksman's book), it is possible to overstress the emphasis placed on the importance of women being in the home. This expectation was for married women. However, despite more jobs for women in shops, offices and the new consumer-goods factories, the inter-war period was not one of expanding employment opportunities for women. Those who did work were still in gender-related employment and the percentage of women who were economically active in 1921 was slightly less than in 1911 and had risen by only 2.5 per cent by 1951.

Another attempt at an overview of women's work is Jane Rendall's *Women in an industrialising society, England 1750–1880* (Basil Blackwell, 1990). Sadly this survey covers only a fraction of the period of *Women's work* but it is a model of what such a survey should be, comprehensive, clear and avoiding the pitfalls of sweeping generalisations by inserting caveats and qualifications where required. Rendall, like many other historians, rightly examines not just women's paid employment but also their work in the home. She questions the assumption that the Industrial Revolution brought rapid changes to women's lives, pointing out that many women continued to do wage-earning work in the home long after the establishment of the first factories. For women who did work outside the home, there is again an analysis of the interaction between their family and working lives.

Bibliography

[1] Sally Alexander, 'Women's Work in Nineteenth-Century London –
A Study of the Years 1820–1850' in [65]. A useful essay for the
beginning of the period about the importance of women's work
which was not recorded by the census.

[2] Sally Alexander, Anna Davin and Eve Hostettler (1979) 'Labouring
Women, a reply to Eric Hobsbawm' in *History Workshop Journal*, 8.
Attacks the stereotype of working-class women being simply wives
and mothers and not workers, Emphasises differences over time and
place.

[3] Alice Amsden (1980) *The Economics of Woman and Work*. An
introduction to the theories of women's work.

[4] W. A. Armstrong (1972) 'The use of information about occupations'
in E. A. Wrigley (ed.), *Nineteenth Century Society*. Not specifically
about women workers but a detailed guide for those wishing to use
the census data.

[5] J. A. Banks (1976) *Prosperity and Parenthood*. Not directly about
working-class women's work but argues that the employment of
servants was part of the 'paraphernalia of gentility' required to
establish middle-class status.

[6] Michelle Barratt and Mary McIntosh (1980) 'The Family Wage:
Some Problems for Socialists and Feminists', *Capital and Class*, No.
11. Contains a counter argument to [46].

[7] J. Benson (1983) *The Penny Capitalists: A Study of Nineteenth Century
Working-Class Entrepreneurs*. A fascinating study of working-class
men and women's enterprise in making both primary and secondary
incomes independently of employers.

[8] Clementina Black (1915) *Married Women's Work Being the Report of
an Enquiry undertaken by the Women's Industrial Council*. A useful
descriptive work; see especially her chapter on rural work and
charwomen.

[9] Board of Trade (1908) *Cost of Living of the Working Classes. Board of*

Trade Enquiry into Working-Class Rents, Housing and Retail Prices in the Principal Industrial Towns, Cmd 3864.

[10] Board of Trade (1931) *The Industrial Survey of Lancashire*. Some interesting material on credit.

[11] Margaret Bondfield (1949) *A Life's Work*. Autobiography of the trade union leader and Labour politician.

[12] *Charles Booth's London; A Portrait of the Poor at the turn of the century* (1969) Drawn from his *Life and Labour of the People of London*. Selected and edited by A. Fried and R. M. Elman. Extracts from Booth's original 17 volumes. Sections on sweating and prostitution and many occupations of London women.

[13] Joanna Bornat (1977) 'Home and Work; A new context for Trade Union history', *Oral History*, 5, No. 2.

[14] Joanna Bornat, 'Lost Leaders, Women, Trade Unionism and the Case of the General Union of Textile Workers 1875–1914' in [51].

[15] Sarah Boston (1980) *Women Workers and the Trade Unions*. Should be read with [56] and [86].

[16] A. L. Bowley (1937) *Wages and Income in the U.K. since 1860*.

[17] Gail Braybon (1981) *Women Workers in the First World War: The British Experience*. Very detailed, essential reading.

[18] Irene Bruegel, 'Women's Employment, Legislation and the Labour Market' in [57]. See also [3].

[19] Sandra Burman (ed.) (1979) *Fit Work for Women*. An interesting and important collection of essays. It includes Kate Purcell, 'Militancy and Acquiescence amongst Women Workers' which analyses women's militancy in trade unions in the 1970s. Useful to compare with the earlier period.

[20] J. Burnett (1974) *Useful Toil*. A very good chapter on domestic servants.

[21] D. Bythell (1978) *The Sweated Trades: Outwork in Nineteenth Century Britain*. Essential reading for the sweated trades.

[22] E. Cadbury, M. Matheson and G. Shann (1909) *Women's Work and Wages*. Information about wages and working conditions taken from interviews with over 6000 women in Birmingham.

[23] Leonore Davidoff, 'The Separation of Home and Work: Landladies and Lodgers in Nineteenth and Twentieth Century England', in [19].

[24] Barbara Drake (1921) *Women in Trade Unions*. An excellent descriptive source for women and trade unions to that date.

[25] Carol Dyhouse (1978) 'Working-class Mothers and Infant Mortality in England 1895–1914', *Journal of Social History*, 12, no. 2. Refutes the long-standing myth of the correlation between high infant mortality rates and high rates of employment for married women.

[26] F. Engels (1845, reprinted 1958) *The Condition of the Working Class*

in England. A classic contemporary survey, data on women workers and working-class living conditions.

[27] R. Floud and D. McCloskey (1981) *The Economic History of Britain since 1700* vol. 1.

[28] W. Hamish Fraser (1981) *The Coming of the Mass Market 1850–1914*. Chapter on credit and useful background to explain the growing demand for shop assistants.

[29] Diana Gittins 'Marital Status, Work and Kinship 1850–1930', in [59]. Shows the complex interconnections between women's work, paid and unpaid, and their familial role.

[30] H. Goldman (1974) *Emma Paterson: Her Life and Times*.

[31] Catherine Hakim (1979) *Occupational Segregation*. Department of Employment Research Paper no. 9. Contains much useful statistical material for the twentieth century.

[32] Catherine Hall, 'The Early Formation of Victorian Domestic Ideology', in [19].

[33] Mary Hamilton (1925) *Mary MacArthur*.

[34] Heidi Hartman (1976) 'Capitalism, Patriarchy and Job Segregation by Sex', in M. Blaxall and B. Regan (eds), *Women and the Workplace*.

[35] R. M. Hartwell (1971) *The Industrial Revolution and Economic Growth*.

[36] Margaret Hewitt (1958) *Victorian Working Wives and Mothers*. Some of the arguments have been refuted (see [25]) but a mass of interesting data on contemporary views (nearly all hostile) to working mothers.

[37] E. Higgs (1982) 'The Tabulation of Occupations in the Nineteenth-Century Census with Special Reference to Domestic Servants', *Local Population Studies*, No. 28.

[38] E. Higgs (1983) 'Domestic Servants and Households in Victorian England', *Social History*, 8, no. 2.

[39] E. Higgs, 'Domestic Service and Household Production', in [51].

[40] Lee Holcombe (1973) *Victorian Ladies at Work: Middle-Class Working Women in England and Wales 1850–1914*. Some references to working-class women, see especially chapters on shop work and clerical workers.

[41] Patricia Hollis (1979) *Women in Public: The Women's Movement 1850–1900*.

[42] Pamela Horn (1975) *The Rise and Fall of the Victorian Servant*. Sees the 'decline' in terms of the rise of alternative work for women.

[43] Pamela Horn (1980) *The Rural World 1750–1850*. Mostly on an earlier period but useful information on the work of rural women in the mid-nineteenth century, especially on crafts and industries.

[44] Eve Hostettler (1977) 'Gourlay Steell and the Sexual Division of Labour', *History Workshop Journal*, no. 4. A short article on the

effects on women's work in agriculture of the introduction of the scythe.

[45] House of Lords Select Committee on Sweating 1888 xxi. Data on women working in the Midlands metal trades and the various sewing and stitching trades.

[46] Jane Humphries (1977) 'Class Struggle and the Persistence of the Working-class Family', *Cambridge Journal of Economics*, 1.

[47] E. H. Hunt (1981) *British Labour History II 1815–1914*.

[48] E. H. Hunt (1973) *Regional Wage Variations in Britain 1850–1914*. Mostly on men's wages but some data on variations in women's wages, also family earnings.

[49] B. L. Hutchins (1915) *Women in Modern Industry*. General survey of women's working conditions.

[50] Angela John (1980) *By the Sweat of Their Brow: Women Workers at Victorian Coal Mines*.

[51] Angela John (ed.) (1986) *Unequal Opportunities: Women's Employment in England 1800–1918*. Essential reading; see especially the introduction.

[52] Jennie Kitteringham, 'Country Work Girls in Nineteenth-century England' in [83].

[53] Viola Klein (1965). *Britain's Married Women Workers*. Results of research done in the 1950s. Interesting data on reasons for women working for wages and effects of work on the family.

[54] K. G. J. Knowles (1952) *Strikes*. A little known work but suggests that women in the inter-war years were more involved in strikes than their numerical involvement in industry would suggest.

[55] Hilary Land, 'Who Still Cares for the Family?', in [57].

[56] Sheila Lewenhak (1977) *Women and Trade Unions*. Should be read in conjunction with [15] and [86].

[57] Jane Lewis (ed.) (1983) *Women's Welfare, Women's Rights*. Deals with contemporary social policy issues covering many aspects of women's lives including employment. Many useful chapters because the issues are set in a historical perspective.

[58] Jane Lewis (1984) *Women in England 1870–1950: Sexual Divisions and Social Change*. Essential reading.

[59] Jane Lewis (ed.) (1986) *Labour and Love: Women's Experience of Home and Family 1850–1940*. More essential reading, especially the introduction.

[60] Jill Liddington and Jill Norris (1978) *One Hand Tied Behind Us; The Rise of the Women's Suffrage Movement*. A lot of interesting material about the working lives of textile women and their involvement both in trade unions and in the suffrage movement.

[61] H. Mayhew (1851, 1967) *London Labour and the London Poor*, 4 vols. Invaluable first-hand accounts of women street sellers, also prostitutes.

[62] Theresa McBride (1976) *The Domestic Revolution.*

[63] N. McKendrick (ed.) (1974) *Historical Perspectives; Studies in English Thought and Society.* See Chapter 3 on the role of women and children in the Industrial Revolution.

[64] S. Meacham (1977) *A Life Apart: The English Working-Class 1890–1914.* A very good general survey.

[65] Juliet Mitchell and Ann Oakley (eds) (1976) *The Rights and Wrongs of Women.*

[66] C. More (1980) *Skill and the English Working-Class 1870–1914.* Investigates the nature of work and the importance of skill and asks if industrial capitalism resulted in deskilling or introduced new skills.

[67] Jenny Morris, 'The Characteristics of Sweating. The late nineteenth century London and Leeds tailoring trade', in [51].

[68] Wanda Neff (1927) *Victorian Working Women 1832–50.* A classic descriptive work.

[69] Sir G. Newman (1906) *Infant Mortality; a social problem.*

[70] Nancy Osterud, 'Gender Divisions and the Organisation of Work in the Leicester Hosiery Industry', in [51].

[71] H. Pelling (1963) *A History of British Trade Unionism.* Virtually nothing on women in trade unions but useful to compare and contrast with [15], [56] and [86].

[72] Maud Pember Reeves (1913) *Round About a Pound a Week.* A survey carried out by Fabian Society's Women's Group of families living on an income of 18–26 shillings a week in South London.

[73] The Pilgrim Trust (1938) *Men Without Work.* An investigation into unemployment and its effects in six areas of England in the 1930s. Includes a chapter on unemployed women and information on women as household managers.

[74] Ivy Pinchbeck (1930) *Women Workers in the Industrial Revolution.*

[75] E. Richards (1974) 'Women in the British Economy since about 1700', *History*, 59.

[76] Elizabeth Roberts (1984) *A Woman's Place: An Oral History of Working-Class Women 1890–1940.*

[77] Elizabeth Roberts (1982) 'Working Wives and their Families', in T. Barker and M. Drake (eds), *Population and Society in Britain 1850–1980.* Lancashire married textile workers.

[78] Elizabeth Roberts, 'Women Strategies', in [59].

[79] Elizabeth Roberts, 'Working-class Family and Social Life', Oral History transcripts of interviews in N. W. England. University of Lancaster.

[80] *Royal Commission on Labour (final Report of)* (1894) c. 7421-1. For information on the sweated trades.

[81] *Royal Commission on Equal Pay 1944–46 (Report of)* cmd. 6937.

[82] R. Seebohm Rowntree (1901) *Poverty: A Study of Town Life*. A seminal study of poverty in York.

[83] R. Samuel (1975) *Village Life and Labour*.

[84] J. Schmiechen (1984) *Sweated Industries and Sweated Labour*.

[85] K. D. M. Snell (1985) *Annals of the Labouring Poor: Social Change in Agrarian England 1600–1900*. Mostly about men but a valuable chapter on women's work; also women's apprenticeships and the family.

[86] N. Soldon (1978) *Women in British Trade Unions 1874–1976*. Should be used in conjunction with [15] and [56].

[87] Margery Spring Rice (1938 and 1981) *Working-Class Wives: Their Health and Conditions*. Contains evidence collected from 1250 questionnaires filled in by working-class wives about their homes, families and health. It is a reminder of how terrible women's conditions could be even in the 1930s.

[88] G. Stedman Jones (1971) *Outcast London*. Includes sweating in the London tailoring and garment trades.

[89] Barbara Taylor (1983) *Eve and the New Jerusalem*. Tailoring trades, but basically about the radical movements of the nineteenth century.

[90] Pam Taylor (1979) 'Daughters and Mothers – Maids and Mistresses: Domestic Service between the Wars', in *Working-Class Culture*, ed. J. Clarke, C. Critchen and R. Johnson.

[91] Melanie Tebbutt (1983) *Making Ends Meet: Pawnbroking and Working-Class Credit*.

[92] Pat Thane *et al* (1984) *The Power of the Past*. Chapter by Joan Scott on men and women in the Parisian garment trade, an interesting comparison with that of London.

[93] Deborah Thom (1978) 'Women at the Woolwich Arsenal 1915–1919', *Oral History*, 6, no. 2.

[94] Deborah Thom, 'The Bundle of Sticks: Women Trade Unionists and Collective Organisation before 1918', in [51].

[95] Louise Tilly and Joan Scott (1978) *Women, Work and Family*. A seminal book looking at the complex and changing inter-relationship between women's familial and labour market role in France and England 1700–1950. Essential reading.

[96] Steve Tolliday (1983) 'Militancy and Organisation, Women Workers and Trade Unions in the Motor Trades in the 1930s', *Oral History*, 11, no. 2.

[97] R. Whipp (1984) 'Plenty of Excuses, No Money', *Society for the Study of Labour History*, 49. Aspects of women's role in the National Society of Pottery Workers, and the interconnection of home, work and union for many women.

[98] Meta Zimmeck, 'Jobs for the Girls: the expansion of clerical work for women 1850–1914', in [51].

Index

New Studies in Economic and Social History

Previously published as

Studies in Economic History

Titles in the series available from the Macmillan Press Limited

Economic History Society

The Economic History Society, which numbers around 3,000 members, publishes the *Economic History Review* four times a year (free to members) and holds an annual conference. Enquiries about membership should be addressed to

The Assistant Secretary
Economic History Society
PO Box 70
Kingswood
Bristol
BS15 5TB

Full-time students may join at special rates.